Negotiating Extra-Territorial Citizenship

Negotiating Extra-Territorial Citizenship

Mexican Migration and the Transnational Politics of Community

David Fitzgerald

CCIS

Center for Comparative Immigration Studies
University of California, San Diego
La Jolla, California

Monograph Series, No. 2
2000

Cover photo: The Colonia Sahuayense marching on December 5, 1999, in their annual procession during the fiesta of the Virgin of Guadalupe. Photo by David Fitzgerald.

Printed in the United States of America

Contents

CHAPTER 4

CHAPTER 5

CHAPTER 6

Figures and Tables

Acknowledgments

This monograph is based on a master's thesis in Latin American Studies at the University of California, San Diego. I am deeply grateful to Wayne Cornelius, director of the Center for Comparative Immigration Studies, for his advice and encouragement. I also thank Yen Espiritu and James Holston for their suggestions on earlier drafts of this work.

Funding for field research was generously provided by the Tinker Foundation. I also thank José Eduardo Zárate Hernández, director of the Center for Anthropological Studies at the Colegio de Michoacán in Zamora. Gail Mummert, Álvaro Ochoa Serrano, Gustavo López Castro, Luis Ramírez Sevilla, Marco Antonio Calderón Mólgora, and Isabel Morales offered advice on site selection and comments on an earlier presentation of the research findings.

Finally, I thank Valeria Godines, my research partner and wife. She supported me in every way during my two years in La Jolla and during our work together in Michoacán and Santa Ana.

Abstract

The dominant nation-state model of citizenship, in which political identity and membership are congruent with state territory, is increasingly unable to resolve the contradictions created by global mass migration. While scholars have studied this problem from the perspective of immigrant-receiving countries, they have paid little attention to citizenship models that would explain how migrants relate to their sending countries. This work draws on evidence from ethnographic fieldwork in Michoacán, Mexico, and Southern California to propose a process-based model of extra-territorial citizenship in which transnational migrants claim citizenship in their places of origin, even when they are physically absent. Legal rights of citizenship, such as voting from abroad, and a kind of moral citizenship in communities of origin share similar theoretical underpinnings. Both forms of citizenship are negotiated with non-migrants who selectively accept or reject the principles of extra-territorial citizenship.

CHAPTER 1

Introduction

"Sahuayans living in the North should come here. This is their house. They should be heard. They should be taken into account!"—*Politician from Sahuayo, Michoacán, member of the Party of the Democratic Revolution (PRD)*

"They were born in Mexico, but they don't like anything here. They are no longer Sahuayans.... They no longer accept Mexico, and Mexico doesn't accept them."—*Businessman in Sahuayo*

"They can't take away our right to vote just because we are here. We are as Mexican as they are."—*Sahuayan businessman in Los Angeles*

Over the last decade, scholars who study migration have increasingly used a transnational lens to describe the flow of people across borders. Previous studies of migration that began with immigrants clambering onto the docks at Ellis Island, or over the wall at San Ysidro, and ended with assimilation into the great American "melting pot" are clearly truncated understandings of a much more complex process. The contemporary migration literature is more likely to pay attention to the ways that migrants maintain ties to both their countries of origin and of destination. The effects of migration on source countries are also a growing field of study. Still, the literature on transnational migration has yet to analyze many aspects of migrants' relationships with their places of origin. The very concept of transnationalism also remains controversial among some social scientists who reject its novelty or usefulness as an analytical tool.

This work aims to contribute to the debates about transnationalism and the political relationships between migrants and their countries and communities of origin. It offers an analytical model to describe the negotiation of "extra-territorial citizenship" that is applicable to a range of forms of citizenship, from the moral to the legal. The model may be used to understand transnational migrant politics on a comparative level, as well as in the case of a single transnational community. It provides a link between the micro and macro levels of transnational politics that is not always clearly explicated in the literature on Mexican migration. I apply this model to specific cases using ethnographic evidence conducted in high-emigration areas of the west-central Mexican state of Michoacán and migrant destination communities in Southern California.

Seventy-five semi-structured interviews were conducted from June 1999 to July 2000 with sending community elites in Michoacán and migrants on both sides of the border currently or formerly involved in transnational organizing. The selection of the primary site of the ethnography, Sahuayo, is in itself significant because Sahuayo is an urban sending site, in contradistinction to the overwhelming emphasis in the Mexican migration literature on rural or small-town sending sites. The transnational political connections between Sahuayo and its U.S. satellites are not formalized in a central institution. Most studies of transnational politics have focused on highly organized migrant associations, thus failing to capture the experiences of less formal and less visible collective migrant practices. This work also makes comparative reference to other Michoacano transnational communities to suggest the tremendous variety of organizational differences that can be understood using the same model.

In chapter 2, I critically discuss basic analytical concepts related to the formation of transnational communities and transnational political participation. I then discuss how transnational migration challenges standard notions of citizenship in the nation-state for both source and destination countries. I propose a model of extra-territorial citizenship to explain one element of the citizenship paradigm that has been under-theorized—how migrants continue to claim citizenship in their country and community of origin even when they are physically absent. The model suggests the cultural and economic bases of the legitimization of extra-territorial citizenship. A competing model of citizenship invoked by some non-migrant elites in Mexico fundamentally rejects or only selectively accepts extra-territorial citizenship.

The question of political transnationalism's novelty is raised in chapter 3. I sketch evidence of high levels of political transnationalism by some European migrants in the late nineteenth and early twentieth centuries before turning to the Mexican case. The dramatic evidence of the involvement of Mexican exiles and laborers in the United States in Mexican politics during the early twentieth century should temper suggestions that political Mexican transnationalism is a new phenomenon. I then describe developments that are more recent in Mexican political transnationalism. My main purpose is not to systematically compare two historical periods, but rather to contextualize the contemporary relationship between Mexican migrants and the state.

Ethnographic evidence from Michoacán is presented in chapters 4 and 5. The negotiation of transnational citizenship is explained first in the case of Sahuayo, where partially overlapping or separate networks organize collective participation of migrants in Sahuayan public life. Some Sahuayan migrants in the United States have organized themselves as the Colonia Sahuayense del Norte (Sahuayan Colony of the North), which sponsors an annual procession in Sahuayo in which returning migrants publicly assert their Sahuayan identity with displays of Mexican and Sahuayan symbols. Sahuayan migrants working through a variety of networks have sponsored projects such as raising funds for a hospital, pharmacy, schoolrooms, and church construction.

The informal nature of such projects is illustrated by the following case from 1999. A mechanic at a Santa Ana, California, garage, who has been shuttling to and from Sahuayo since 1971, fixed cars and slept on the shop floor during the workweek to save money to build his house in Sahuayo. On weekends, he reverted to his role as president of a volunteer paramedic corps in Sahuayo and sought out other Sahuayan migrants for contributions to buy an ambulance. He showed them a photograph of a second-hand 1988 Ford ambulance driving in a parade of migrants through the streets of Sahuayo with a poster taped to the rear window thanking the "colony and family of Sahuayans living in the United States." A priest in Santa Ana refused to allow fund-raising for the project at his church, but the mechanic finally raised $5,000 for the ambulance among a network of Sahuayan friends. After raising the money, the mechanic spent three months negotiating with Mexican government agencies, the city of Santa Ana, and Mexican migrant civic associations before he was able to bring the ambulance to Sahuayo. The $5,000 ambulance may not seem like a major purchase, but it is the only ambulance serving the public in a town of 60,000. Two years after buying the ambulance, the mechanic was back in Santa Ana seeking more donations.

A discussion of these and other projects reveals tensions among migrants, Mexican government officials, and diverse elements within the Catholic Church that can expand or limit the possibilities of citizenship negotiations. Local politicians are increasingly reaching out to Sahuayan migrants, but the current limits of migrant participation in electoral politics are revealed in the July 2000 presidential and congressional elections, in which only returned or shuttle migrants appeared to play a substantive role.

In chapter 5, comparative evidence from the neighboring town of Jiquilpan demonstrates a more institutionalized relationship between migrants and the state. The triadic relationship forged between Jiquilpense migrants, the Mexican state, and the U.S. state is upheld by some Sahuayan politicians as an exemplary model. The mayor of Jiquilpan visits the association of Jiquilpenses in Inglewood, California, once or twice a year to encourage association support for community development and philanthropic projects in Jiquilpan. Migrants have also served as a liaison in the establishment of a sister-city relationship between Jiquilpan and Inglewood. Finally, evidence from the Michoacano village of El Granjenal demonstrates a third model of transnational political organization in which the political structure of the village is tightly bound with migrant life in the destination city of Santa Ana. Migrants have radically transformed the village's infrastructure, and the two elected leaders of El Granjenal divide their time equally between Santa Ana and El Granjenal.

I conclude with some further observations about the theoretical tensions in extra-territorial citizenship that are not addressed by the subjects of the ethnography. I propose that the research agenda for transnationalism must take into consideration how cultural and economic practices and attitudes inform transnational politics at both the macro and micro levels. Finally, I analyze the July 2000 election of Vicente Fox as president of Mexico and the Institutional Revolutionary Party's (PRI) loss of control in the federal Senate to suggest how a new political environment may influence a range of citizenship practices on the micro level.

CHAPTER 2

Theories of Transnationalism and Extra-Territorial Citizenship

Transnational Communities

A burgeoning literature in immigration studies over the past decade suggests that many migrants to the United States are constructing transnational identities that challenge standard bipolar notions of immigration in which emigrants definitively leave one country and become settled immigrants in another (Rouse 1989, Glick Schiller et al. 1992). The questions raised by a transnational approach can lead to a better understanding of how migrants interact and identify with multiple nations, states, and communities. However, the very concept of transnationalism is fiercely debated by scholars who are rethinking—or at times resisting rethinking—basic social science concepts such as citizenship, identity, and nationalism (Mummert 1999, Goldring 1996). Transnationalism has been criticized on both empirical and theoretical grounds. Portes and his colleagues warn that "if all or most things that immigrants do are defined as 'transnationalism', then none is because the term becomes synonymous with the total set of experiences of this population" (Portes et al. 1999: 219). This essay avoids that definitional pitfall by focusing on a narrowly defined slice of transnational practices—collective action by migrants in the public life of their community of origin.

Scholars who refer to transnationalism do not always share a precise definition of the term. Appadurai describes transnationalism as primarily a cultural phenomenon in which global capital has created practices and meanings that are no longer bound to a geographic place (1991). Transnationalism is also used to refer to what were formerly known as multinational corporations and are now called "transnational" to emphasize the diffuse sites of production, sales, and capital sources that form the corporation (Rouse 1995). Transnationalism as used in this essay is a more restricted term proposed by Basch and others who define transnationalism as "the processes by which immigrants forge and sustain multi-stranded social relations that link together their societies of origin and settlement." These processes are called transnational "to emphasize that many immigrants today build social fields that cross geographic, cultural, and political borders" (Basch et al. 1994: 7). Transnational practices may take place in localities such as transborder communities of migrants or in the mobile space of the traveling migrant, but transnational practices are always situated in a social space, even when that space is not static.

Terms such as "community of origin" that are set in dichotomous opposition to "community of destination" are sometimes considered problematic in a transnational conceptual framework. In a "transnational community" (R. Smith 1995), "transnational migration circuit" (Rouse 1989), or "transnational social field" (Basch et al. 1994), social formations are not bifurcated by national boundaries. The sending/receiving and home/host dichotomies have the same definitional problems as origin/destination.[1] For example, the child of Mexican immigrants born in the U.S. "destination site" might then move to a Mexican "site of origin," thus upsetting the directional flow implicit in the definition. On a historical and macro level, however, there are dominant directional flows that make these terms useful, even when there is a single imagined community for many transnational migrants. There is also an important distinction to make between sites of origin and destination to develop a vocabulary for comparative analysis. Therefore, I use terms such as "site of origin" and "site of destination" while recognizing their potential imperfections to describe the histories of individual migrants. I use the term "transnational communities" rather than other formulations with similar shades of meaning because community lies at the heart of the questions of membership addressed in the study.

The literature on transnational migration has generally been concerned with introducing a sense of migrant agency into migration studies (Mummert 1999, Basch et al. 1994). While this is a laudable goal, the discussion of migrants' claims-making concerning their places of origin has generally understated the dialogic nature of membership. Ríos criticizes a number of transnational

---

[1] The sending/receiving dichotomy also has been criticized for denying the agency of migrants who are not "sent" by anyone but themselves. However, these terms illuminate the international capitalist system that structures the decisions of individual migrants, much like the distinction between labor-exporting and labor-importing countries.

studies in Glick Schiller and her colleagues' edited volume (1992) for their inattention to the experiences of migrants' families and associates who never leave the sending community. Ríos asks if they also experience something equivalent to transnationalism. This crucial question has not been addressed adequately on an empirical level. The bipolar model of sending and receiving communities by itself is obviously incapable of explaining transnational practices and imaginations of community, but the exclusive use of "transnational community" assumes that non-migrants in a sending site are part of transnational processes. Though non-migrants may in fact be deeply influenced by transnational practices and "social remittances" (Levitt 1998), their imagined communities are not necessarily transnational. For the actors in areas of high migration, there are communities of origin and destination, as well as the potential for a transnational community. These are communities with overlapping, fluid boundaries whose members live in multiple physical sites.

To clarify the relationship between social identity and physical space, I use "community" to mean an imagined group of members who share a collective identity (B. Anderson 1991). Collective community identity does not suggest a uniformity of its members' interests, because all communities are fractured to at least some extent along lines of gender, age, and class (Levitt 1999). Communities are often based on attachments to a geographic place, but those communities can include members who do not inhabit the place. A community's boundaries are ambiguous and subject to negotiation by its members. Much of the postmodern literature on transnationalism celebrates the delinking of space from identity (Glick Schiller et al. 1992, Mahler 1998, Sorenson 1998), yet the importance of place to identity formation should not be overlooked. Transnational identities are formed by emotional, political, and social attachments to specific places where the substantive practices of citizenship are enacted.

Transnational Practices as Resistance?

Glick Schiller, Basch, and Blanc-Szanton view migrants' subjugated ethnic and class positions in the United States and their countries of origin as fundamentally linked to their transnational practices (1992). They acknowledge that class positions can change as migrants move between multiple sites. Despite this acknowledgment, which becomes stronger in their later work (Basch et al.

1994, Glick Schiller and Fouron 1999), Glick Schiller and her associates are clearly hopeful that "transmigrants" will use their transnationality to challenge the hegemony of global capitalism (1992). Smith and Guarnizo warn against celebrating transnational migrant practices. They caution that researchers should not impute "resistance" to actions that are not political or self-consciously resistant. In many cases, transnational actors may enthusiastically participate in hegemonic projects rather than resist them. A wealth of empirical evidence suggests that migrants are more likely to attempt to accumulate capital themselves rather than challenge the entire capitalist order (M. Smith and Guarnizo 1998).

Basch and her colleagues also see transnationalism as a locus for resistance against racialization and ethnic discrimination. This argument is supported by comparative evidence from a wide range of migrant experiences described in their edited volume (Basch et al. 1994) and elsewhere. For example, Haitian migrants in New York City resist their identification with marginalized African-Americans by maintaining ties to Haiti. The migrants also resist their incorporation into the political project of African-American politicians for the same reason. The latter see transnational ties as a threat to building African-American political power in New York. By distancing themselves, Haitians are resisting being lumped together in U.S. racial categories at the same time as they are accommodating the hegemonic subordination of African-Americans. In R. C. Smith's 1995 study, Mexican migrants in New York City similarly resisted their identification with other minority groups such as Puerto Ricans by strengthening their ties to their community in Mexico. Assertions of ethnic identity may not challenge white privilege so much as they reinforce it through interethnic conflict among marginalized groups.

Smith and Guarnizo differentiate between transnationalism "from above" and "from below." Grassroots transnational practices by migrants rise from below, unlike transnational practices from above, epitomized by the policies of the state or transnational corporations. The authors acknowledge that this distinction is sometimes difficult to make. For instance, are wealthy Chinese immigrant entrepreneurs who use transnational linkages engaging in practices from above or below (Smart and Smart 1998)? The shifting class positions made possible by transnational movement also demonstrate the limitations of the above/below dichotomy, as Mahler underlines with examples of Salvadoran migrants who are wage laborers in the United States and exploiters of wage labor in El Salvador.

Smith and Guarnizo assert that transnationalism is not a "thing" that can be readily "measured," so they discourage the conception of a person or group as "more or less transnational" (1998). Yet the thickness of transnational ties in a social formation is a crucial question in the assessment of the formation's effects and prospects for durability. While such "positivist taxonomies" may not always easily frame empirical evidence, it is inconsistent for the authors to call for comparative work while rejecting analytical measures of transnationality that can be applied to diverse cases.

Transnationalism, Citizenship, and the Nation-State

The ideal type of the nation-state is a polity where the boundaries of an ethno-cultural nation are congruent with the boundaries of state territory (Gellner 1983). Some nations cross state boundaries, such as the German *volk* that is divided between Germany, Austria, and neighboring states (Brubaker 1989). Many states—such as Spain, which includes Catalonians and Basques—are composed of multiple nationalities. There are few nation-states that firmly adhere to the ideal type, but the nation-state nevertheless remains a standard of the international system. Immigration further complicates the nation-state model when immigrants of different nationalities enter the state's territory. These immigrants may live in the territory for generations without becoming citizens, thus creating a disjuncture between residence and membership in the polity (Brubaker 1992).

Soysal has argued for a post-national model of citizenship based on universal citizenship and the devolution of state power to supra-national arrangements such as the European Union (EU). Non-citizen residents of a state can claim civil, social, and even limited political rights, based on discourses of universal personhood. National identity is no longer linked to the right to make claims on the polity (Soysal 1994). Soysal has identified an important shift in the citizenship politics of the EU, but even within the EU the severance of the link between identity and claims-making is far from universally accepted. The applicability of the post-national model beyond the special case of the EU is even more limited. Citizenship in many cases around the world depends on essentialized identities that legitimate rights claims. Although the concept of nations as "imagined communities" (B. Anderson 1991) and "invented traditions" (Hobsbawm 1990) is widely accepted among social scientists, essentialized conceptions of nationality are often the rule among policy elites and the public.

Essentialized national identities and "museum-ized" memories of the homeland are especially strong among diasporans and transnational migrants (Tölölyan 1996: 14, Das Gupta 1997). At the same time, transnational migrants challenge nation-state models of citizenship in both sending and receiving countries by moving back and forth between states, sometimes circumventing state controls over borders and taxes (N. Rodríguez 1996). Transnational migrants often live in a country in which they do not claim citizenship and claim citizenship in a country in which they do not live. Alternately, they may claim membership in multiple polities in which they may be residents, part-time residents, or absentees. Transnational migration challenges both sending and receiving states' exclusive claim on a migrant's loyalty (Hammar 1989). Models of citizenship that consider immigration are primarily constructed by scholars from countries of immigration who are studying the implications for their own or other receiving countries. The transnational implications of citizenship are not fully considered. This monograph addresses the largely missing half of a model of transnational citizenship—citizenship by transnational migrants in their countries of origin.

Negotiating Extra-Territorial Citizenship

Extra-territorial citizenship is citizenship in a territorially bounded political community without residence in the community. It also may be citizenship in the territorially unbounded imagined community of citizens with a common attachment to a place of origin. By extra-territorial citizenship, I do not only mean the rights and obligations of legal citizenship. Citizenship has a moral dimension that is not always congruent with legal status. The extra-territorial citizenship claims I found in my case study of Sahuayo are primarily moral, though the principles underlying these claims also are reflected in the national and transnational debate in Mexico over legal extra-territorial citizenship rights.

One manifestation of extra-territorial citizenship is citizenship in a territorially unbounded imagined community. Citizenship in diasporic communities such as the dispersed nations of Jews, Palestinians, and Armenians falls under this definition. Mexicans abroad are not, strictly speaking, a diaspora. They have not been forcibly expelled from their ancestral home, they are able to return if they desire, and they do not necessarily see their ancestral home as a place of eventual return. All diasporas wax and wane in their congruence to an ideal diasporic type, but many Mexicans abroad today have diasporic elements such as longing, a collective memory of the homeland, and dis-identification with the "host" country (Clifford 1994). Membership in a diasporic or transnational community is probably necessary for an absentee before even considering claiming membership in the place of origin, but I will concentrate here on extra-territorial citizenship as the assertion of citizenship in the place of origin.

Extra-territorial citizenship is similar to Holston's concept of "urban citizenship" in its location of the city (or village) as the locus of the practices and claims-making of citizenship (Holston n.d.1). The two concepts share a focus on the moral rather than the legal dimension of citizenship. Yet extra-territorial citizenship is the inverse of urban citizenship in a crucial sense. The Mexican immigrants Holston describes in Oceanside, California, can claim "urban citizenship" in Oceanside based on their residence in the city, even if they are not American citizens. Absentee Sahuayans claiming extra-territorial citizenship in Sahuayo are claiming citizenship because they are "good" Sahuayans and Mexicans, even if they are not residents of Sahuayo.

Membership is claimed by a public affirmation of identity. An affirmation by itself is not sufficient to achieve membership. Membership in a community is only achieved when other members of the community recognize an identity claim as legitimate (Taylor 1992). In other words, membership is achieved through the negotiation of (re)affirmations and confirmations of a collective identity. This is a negotiation over the formal aspect of membership. "Formal" does not necessarily describe a legal standing, but rather "the status of membership in a political community ... [that] establishes who is and who is not a citizen, who owes allegiance to that community and is owed protection by it" (Holston n.d.2).

Membership status is dynamic. It is subject to challenge and negotiation, especially in the context of transnational migration, where potential community members are often physically absent from the site of origin. Membership is also uneven. The outcome of (re)affirmations and recognitions of membership is expressed in different levels of membership. The levels range from full enjoyment of civil, political, and social rights (Marshall 1992) to symbolic membership with none of the Marshallian rights. By symbolic membership, I mean a recognized affirmation of collective identity that makes no claims on other members of the community.

Is membership necessarily citizenship? Citizenship is a subset of membership, sometimes described as membership in a political community (Oldfield 1998). Symbolic membership by itself does not qualify as citizenship, because symbolic membership is not political. Symbolic members are not claiming to be part of a polity. They are claiming to be members of a community that may have overlapping membership with the polity. For example, in Gans's estimation, third- and fourth-generation Americans who assert a "symbolic ethnicity" declare their identity "by 'affiliating' with an abstract collectivity which does not exist as an interacting group. That collectivity ... can be mythic or real, contemporary or historical." Distant homelands are especially attractive "identity symbols" because "they cannot make arduous demands on American ethnics." Neither do symbolic ethnics make demands on the homeland (Gans 1979). Symbolic membership is not an assertion of citizenship unless it is accompanied by claims to the rights held by other citizens. A citizen is a member of a community who makes claims on other members and whose right to make claims is accepted by other members of the community. Making claims on other members is inherently political.[2]

Fundamentally, citizenship is the right to protection both from and by the political community (Holston n.d.2). The right to protection is a resource that is contested, given that the right to protection is necessarily accompanied by the community's obligation to protect. The community that accepts other individuals or a group as citizens is undertaking an obligation to protect them and allow them the capacity to have an effective presence in the public space. In its moral essence, citizenship is the capacity to be heard (Balibar 1988). Sahuayan migrants who participate in the public space of Sahuayo, even when they are physically absent most of the year, are asserting extra-territorial citizenship. They are asking to be "taken into account" by non-migrant members of the community. In Balibar's terms, they are demanding an effective presence in the public space.

---

[2] My assessment of whether a practice is "political" follows Leftwich (1983). Politics exists in every realm of social life. "Political" action consists of the negotiation or contestation of power for controlling the production and distribution of resources. Resources include not only physical capital and goods, but also social and human capital.

To be taken into account means that one's interests are pro-
tected even during periods of absence. In the context of transnational migration, the protection of interests includes private and
public property rights and inclusive cultural rights. Private property rights are the rights to the protection of property such as land
and houses. Throughout Mexico, communities with historically
high emigration rates are filled with empty houses that are only
occupied when migrants return for vacation or retirement (Massey
et al. 1987). Even many "settled immigrants" in receiving countries
continue to view sending sites as centers for rest and relaxation or
retirement (Cornelius 1990, Mines 1981). Public property rights
include the right to participate in decisions that affect public infrastructure. Absentees often continue to have an interest in the
development of the town, which is expressed through patronage
of infrastructure projects such as paving roads, building community centers, repairing cathedrals, and developing potable water
systems (Goldring 1998, R. Smith 1995).

The right to be taken into account is also a cultural right. It is
not a cultural right in Young's sense of "differentiated citizenship"
(1989) which gives a social group special treatment in order to
protect its difference (Kymlicka 1995, Taylor 1992). Rather, it is an
inclusive cultural right that asks for similar treatment based on a
shared identity. Unlike the property interests that can be expressed through law as well as a moral code, this cultural right is
purely a moral right. It is the right to be welcomed as a "good"
member of the community, even after a period of extended absence in a foreign cultural milieu. Returnees who are taken into
account are accepted as moral citizens because they share a cultural identity with non-migrants. Identity is negotiated in the public space of migrant sending sites like Sahuayo through displays
such as the parades of returning migrants that are discussed in
chapter 4.

Migrant economic participation in the community is another
potential legitimization of extra-territorial citizenship claims.
Shklar describes how economic participation has historically been
a necessary condition of full citizenship in the United States.
Working outside the home and paying taxes are the primary forms
of economic participation that legitimate status as a "good" citizen
(1991). Economic participation in the form of remittances can legitimate citizenship claims in the context of migration. Annual
migrant remittances to Mexico are difficult to quantify given that
many remittances are pocket transfers rather than money orders or
banking transactions. Lozano Ascencio estimated remittances to be

$3.4 billion in 1990, then equal to Mexico's income from foreign tourism and only slightly less than income from the *maquiladora* industry (1993). A Banco de México report in April 2000 estimated that annual remittances increased from $3.7 billion in 1995 to almost $6 billion in 1999. A report released in March 2000 by the National Population Council (CONAPO) in Mexico estimated that only three-fourths of the remittance flow was captured by the Banco de México study. The CONAPO study estimated annual remittances of $8 billion, which provided essential economic support to 1.1 million households in Mexico (*SourceMex* 2000). Regardless of the precise figures, remittances are widely accepted to be an important segment of the Mexican economy, particularly in sending areas of west-central Mexico (Massey et al. 1987). Sending remittances is considered a sign of continued interest and involvement in the community.

Extra-territorial citizenship appeals to a Roman-like model of citizenship. Opposing notions of citizenship, asserted by some non-migrants who reject extra-territorial citizenship, appeal to a Greek tradition of civic-republicanism. The extra-territorial model is not Roman-like in the sense of a juridical citizenship, but rather because it shares several basic principles. These same principles resonate in the national Mexican debate over the extension of legal rights of citizenship to Mexicans abroad. Similar features of the extra-territorial and Roman models include passivity, citizenship as right, protection of property, and differentiation (Pocock 1998).

Like the Roman model, extra-territorial citizenship is relatively passive. Although the extra-territorial model requires the periodic performance of membership claims through remittances or public identity displays—as the Greek model also demands—on a daily basis, extra-territorial citizenship is necessarily passive. The ruled do not rule as they would in an Aristotelian system, because they are absent. In the extra-territorial model, citizenship is also a right that is "owed." Citizens are owed protection by their community because they were born there. Sahuayans abroad claim they deserve protection of their private and public property because they are Sahuayans. Citizenship is also differentiated. The individual and the communities to which the individual makes claims negotiate multiple levels of simultaneous citizenships. For example, Sahuayans abroad may be moral or legal citizens of Santa Ana, California, and the United States, and at the same time be moral or legal citizens of Sahuayo, Michoacán, and Mexico.

Non-migrants who reject extra-territorial citizenship claims appeal to a Greek model of citizenship in which citizenship is participatory, based on duty as well as rights, and territorially bound (Pocock 1998, Oldfield 1998). Under this model, citizenship is based on daily participation in the polis. Political participation cannot be a right without commensurate public duties. Because migrants are physically outside the polity, it is impossible to co-erce them into fulfilling their obligations. Absent migrants cannot be citizens in an Aristotelian sense because of their very absence. The tension between these two models of citizenship can be found in national-level politics in Mexico as well as in sending communities in Michoacán.

CHAPTER 3

Mexican Political Transnationalism in Historical Perspective

Is Political Transnationalism New?

One of the criticisms of the concept of transnationalism is that it does not describe anything new. If transnationalism is not new, the argument goes, there is no need to further clutter the terminology and models of the social sciences when existing paradigms are adequate (Portes et al. 1999). The present work is not a historical study that can definitively answer the question of transnationalism's novelty. Several conclusions can be drawn from the evidence in this chapter, however. It appears that transnationalism is not so much a new phenomenon, but that American ideologies of assimilation and even multiculturalism have obscured the transnationality of earlier immigrant practices which are only recently being theorized as transnational.

The dominant historiography of American immigration has been that immigrants arrive in the United States and shed their Old Country identities, languages, and practices over the course of one or two generations. Immigrants assimilate into the American "melting pot" and become virtually indistinguishable from other Americans. This historiography has a strong normative component in which assimilation has not only been the historical experience of American immigrants; it is the only way immigrants *should* behave if the United States is to remain a viable nation-state that does not disintegrate along ethno-cultural lines (see Zolberg 1996). The position that cultural assimilation is necessary to make moral claims on political citizenship suggests the subordination of minority or nonconformist groups (Carens 1989). A more pluralist conception of immigration has taken root since the 1960s Civil Rights movement. According to a "multiculturalist" model of American citizenship, it is acceptable for immigrants to hold plural cultural identities so long as they remain exclusively loyal politically to one American nation (Walzer 1992). Transnationalism challenges both the assimilationist and multicultural models by asserting the possibility of multiple loyalties and identities (Glick Schiller et al. 1992). Political identities are not neatly severed from culture. Assertions of cultural identity themselves become political.

Immigrants from a variety of nationalities and different historical periods have engaged in transnational practices. Transnationalism is not particular to Mexican migrants, so transnationalism cannot only be explained as a unique case in U.S. immigration history arising from the geographic proximity of Mexico. In his discussion of Polish, Jewish, and Irish immigrants, Jacobson writes that "American historians tend to write about immigration as arrival and settlement, but the migrants themselves often experienced the move—and the weight of emigrant cultures' perpetually enforced interpretation of the move—as departure and *absence*." This mind-set has important consequences regardless of a physical return. "The diasporic imagination ... often has more to do with how one sees and thinks about the world than with where one ultimately chooses to live in it" (Jacobson 1995: 2, 9).

Irish emigrants were often given an "American wake" to bid them a ritualized farewell because they were never expected to return. Yet once in the United States, they often became active in transnational politics. Even if they were forced to migrate for ostensibly economic reasons, many Irish immigrants during the late nineteenth and early twentieth centuries considered themselves exiles and were deeply involved in the Irish national liberation project. In 1867, former Fenian rebels from Ireland working for Irish independence established the Clan na Gael, with local branches around the United States to coordinate with rebels in Ireland for an armed Irish revolt. The Irish Revolutionary Brotherhood also established chapters throughout the United States. Less extremist Irish-American organizations such as the Irish National League were more gradualist and sought Irish autonomy through moral and economic contributions to their compatriots in Ireland. The transnational strength of Irish nationalism depended on events in both the United States and Ireland. The rise of American nativism in the 1890s fueled the flames of Irish nationalism directed at Irish independence as well as improving the position of Irish Americans.[3] After the "Troubles" began in the six counties of the North in 1969, the Irish Republican Army formed sixty-two

---

[3] Similarly, the anti-immigrant climate in California in the early 1990s created a backlash of Mexican ethnic and national identification (Portes 1999).

chapters around the United States which raised funds and political support.

The Irish case is but one of several examples of immigrant involvement in national liberation projects. Similar organizations of Polish immigrants, such as the liberationist Polish National Alliance and the more moderate nationalist Polish Roman Catholic Union, had 40,000 members in twenty-two states by the end of the nineteenth century (Jacobson 1995). Hungarians, Lithuanians, Czechs, and other immigrants have a long history of transnational politics (Glick Schiller 1999). Immigrants from diverse origins have also organized in the United States to provide mutual aid to other immigrants from a common town of origin. For example, Italians and Poles often created associations based on their devotion to their hometown's patron saint or Virgin (R. Smith 1998a, Orsi 1985, Jacobson 1995). Migrants from Eastern and Southern Europe formed hometown associations (HTAs) that improved churches, cemeteries, schools, and public works in migrants' places of origin (Glick Schiller 1999). Hometown ties of the latter sort are not really new, but they have only recently been recognized in the literature on transnationalism (see Glick Schiller et al. 1992).

The Transnational Politics of Mexico and Its Migrants

Although transnational political practices were much more dramatic among Mexicans in the United States ninety years ago than they are today, the forms of the practices have changed in important ways. The small body of literature that describes the historical relations between Mexico and Mexicans in the United States often does not distinguish between elite political exiles, migrant workers, and people of Mexican descent born in U.S. territory (Chicanos). This imprecision is not necessarily a failure of scholarship but rather a reflection of historical conditions. In Los Angeles, "The generation of American-born Mexican Americans ... did not emerge as an influential factor in the city's history until their maturation during the Depression decade" (Sánchez 1993: 254). Armando Gutiérrez claims that until the 1940s, the Mexican government generally made little distinction between Mexican citizens and Chicanos (1986: 47).[4]

---

[4] However, in 1911 the Mexican consulate in Laredo, Texas, drew sharp distinctions between Mexicans and Americans of Mexican descent (Gómez-Quiñones 1973).

The Mexican Revolution provides the strongest evidence of interactions between Mexicans on both sides of the border. Oaxacan anarchist Ricardo Flores Magón organized the Mexican Liberal Party (PLM) in 1905 with the stated goal of overthrowing Porfirio Díaz. Local chapters formed throughout Arizona, Texas, and California, where the PLM collected funds and recruited men among Chicanos and Mexican migrant workers (Gómez-Quiñones 1973, Santamaría Gómez 1994). Mexican consulates in the United States responded with physical assaults and campaigns of intimidation, often coordinated with U.S. authorities. Street fighting between pro– and anti–PLM forces broke out in Los Angeles and San Diego (Gómez-Quiñones 1973).

When the Mexican Revolution began in 1910, cross-border raids from anti-*porfirista* forces in Texas had a twenty-year history in the area. General Torres of the Mexican army remarked that "the problem would be resolved very quickly if it were not for the help the rebels receive in Texas." After Madero took office, the *maderista* consul in El Paso openly recruited men as soldiers until he fled U.S. officials who were selectively enforcing neutrality laws. Venustiano Carranza later recruited men in Laredo, El Paso, Los Angeles, San Antonio, San Diego, and Calexico (Gómez Quiñones 1973).

Supported by the Mexican consulates, revolutionary clubs formed in U.S. border cities in 1915. A constitutionalist newspaper financed by the consul in San Diego called on the clubs to petition the Wilson administration to recognize the Carranza regime—generations before the idea of Chicanos as an ethnic lobby came into vogue. The following year, the Mexican government asked Mexicans in the United States to register at the consulates. A San Antonio newspaper explained the government's motivation. "The principal reason for the register is to see on which side lie the sympathies of Mexicans living in the United States, in case there is an uprising" (Gómez Quiñones 1973: 40, my translation).

Following the Revolution, the Mexican consulate remained deeply involved in the affairs of the Mexican community in Los Angeles. The consul organized the Federation of Mexican Workers Union in 1928 and organized mutual aid societies, or *mutualistas*, into the Confederation of Mexican Societies. Although the mutualistas were primarily concerned with providing services like funerals to their members, the Confederation joined the consulate in supporting repatriation and the restriction of Mexican immigration. Nationalists in Mexico had long seen mass emigration as an affront to the nation-building process following the Revolution.

Consular officials also encouraged the repatriation of Mexicans in the hope that the skills they had acquired in the North would help build the Mexican state. The consulate arranged reduced train fares for Mexican repatriates and distributed flyers in Los Angeles calling on "Mexico's sons" to return. When the United States began deporting Mexicans and urging their "voluntary repatriation" during the Great Depression, the Mexican consulate cooperated with U.S. authorities. Over a third of the Mexican population of Los Angeles returned to Mexico. As a result, the remaining population shifted toward a second generation of more homogenous blue-collar workers oriented toward political action in the United States rather than Mexico (Sánchez 1993). The Mexican government further restrained the consulate's involvement in the political and social affairs of Los Angeles's Mexican community, and the influence of the consulate began a long decline (Balderrama 1982).

Mexican presidential candidates visited the Mexican community in the United States as early as 1928, when José Vasconcelos campaigned throughout the Southwest, urging Mexicans to repatriate to Mexico (Sánchez 1993). Thousands gathered to hear him speak in Los Angeles, and clubs formed around the United States to promote his candidacy. When Pascual Ortiz Rubio won the election, *vasconcelistas* in the United States in the Anti-Reelection Party and the Non-Partisan Committee for Mexican Elections publicly charged the Mexican government with fraud and protested to the U.S. Department of State (Santamaría Gómez 1994). Six years later, 40,000 Mexicans joined a procession in Los Angeles to celebrate the Virgin of Guadalupe and protest *cardenista* persecution of the Catholic Church in Mexico. The political message behind an ostensibly religious procession was explicitly expressed by its organizers. The Mexican consul urged Mexicans to boycott the procession and denounced the organizers as "a group of persons ... already well known as the traditional enemies of the economic, social, and cultural progress of Mexico" (Sánchez 1993).

Clearly, transnational political action is not new in the Mexican case. Although there was little political contact between Mexicans in the United States and the Mexican government in the 1950s and 1960s (Bustamante 1986), Mexicans and Chicanos held demonstrations outside the Mexican consulate in Los Angeles to protest the massacre of students at the Plaza de Tlatelolco in Mexico City in 1968 (Santamaría Gómez 1994). When Luis Echeverría assumed the presidency in 1970, he reached out to Chicanos in hopes of motivating them as an ethnic lobby and repairing his image as an architect of the 1968 Tlatelolco massacre. The foreign service elite generally disdained working-class migrants and Chicanos, deriding the latter as *pochos*, or "gringo-ized" Mexicans. A series of meetings between Mexican presidents from Echeverría through José López Portillo (1976–1982) and Miguel de la Madrid (1982–1988) took place with a Chicano elite rather than with Mexican migrants (Gutiérrez 1986).

It was not until 1988 that relations between the Mexican government and Mexican migrants began to change substantially. What has changed is the sustained opposition organizing among Mexican-born migrants in the United States and the way the PRI has institutionalized its U.S. presence in response (Guarnizo 1998). In 1988, Cuauhtémoc Cárdenas (who founded the PRD the following year) campaigned in California in his failed bid to upset PRI presidential candidate Carlos Salinas de Gortari.

> Mexicans living in the United States, many of whom were driven from their homeland by economic and political problems, have become a natural constituency for Cárdenas. Cardenismo encountered fertile ground across the border because it appealed—as in Mexico— to the discontented and disaffected. Mexicans in the U.S. harbor great resentment against a political and economic system in their home country that has been unable (or unwilling) to absorb them into the formal economy or to assure them effective political representation (Dresser 1993: 96).

The Mexican consul in Los Angeles, José Ángel Pescador, acknowledged in 1991 that the 1988 Cárdenas campaign was a turning point in the PRI's relationship with the migrant population.

> One of the greatest protest marches against the outcome of the elections took place in Los Angeles. This led to an awakening in Mexican political circles. The Mexican government realized that there are many anti–PRI Mexicans living in California who return periodically to their communities and have influence in Mexico. This recognition took place in the context of a radical reformulation of Mexico's foreign policy. What we want to do now is build bridges with the Mexican community (in Dresser 1993: 94).

There were four main motives that drove the Mexican state to strengthen its ties with its citizens abroad. These included circumventing the outreach of the opposition PRD among Mexicans living in the United States, encouraging Mexicans in the United States to participate in U.S. politics as an ethnic lobby, and stimulating the flow of remittances. The fourth motive was to protect the civil rights of Mexican citizens in a hostile U.S. political environment where Mexicans were subject to abuses by the U.S. Border Patrol and anti-immigrant political initiatives such as California's Proposition 187. The Mexican state's strategy has led to a negotiation of extra-territorial citizenship initiated from above, rather than the grassroots forms of extra-territorial citizenship initiated from below in Sahuayo.

The Mexican government began to build those bridges through initiatives such as the Program for Mexican Communities Abroad (PACME), created in 1990 under the Ministry of Foreign Relations (SRE). The very name of the program asserts the Mexican national identity of Mexicans in the United States by contrasting it with their residence abroad. Solidarity International, the international arm of President Salinas's National Solidarity Program (PRONASOL), was created two years later. Both programs formalized arrangements between U.S.–based migrant organizations and Mexican federal, state, and local governments in order to carry out public works projects in sending communities. Projects were initiated both by U.S.–based migrants and by residents and authorities of the sending communities (Pérez Godoy 1992).

The Solidarity projects were conceived in the larger context of the Salinas and Ernesto Zedillo (1994–2000) regimes' restructuring of center-periphery relations carried out under the rubric of "new federalism." In his doctoral dissertation and subsequent work, Carlos Salinas wrote that communities that participated in their own development tended to form highly critical attitudes toward the government. Salinas proposed that a decentralized development program that involved local community leaders in the decision-making process would be less corrupt and more responsive to local needs. The rural sector could be developed economically while simultaneously generating support for the federal government (Salinas de Gortari 1982: 39–42).

The National Solidarity Program that Salinas initiated upon assuming the presidency allowed for a relatively higher level of local participation in selecting and developing public projects, even as the design of the program, funding levels, and major decisions were controlled by the central government (Cornelius et al.

1994: 21). Martínez Saldaña asserts that Solidarity International and the PACME were created and implemented in an authoritarian fashion and devoid of migrant participation in the decision-making process (1993: 15). Likewise, Pérez Godoy sees the programs as an acknowledgment of migrants' economic rights in their sending country but a restriction on their political participation (1998: 144–45). However, economic and political participation cannot always be separated, frequently to the frustration of government officials whose political purposes are at odds with those of the migrants. Economic participation may be used to justify access to political power. As a PRD official for Cárdenas's 2000 campaign in California explained, "There's a whole channel of communication that's under the radar screen with Mexicans here and in Mexico." In sending money back, "part of the message we send to Mexico is, 'Vote for me'" (Sheridan 2000).

Ernesto Zedillo further legitimated the participation of U.S.–based Mexicans in Mexican political life through his National Development Plan 1995–2000, which declared that "the Mexican Nation extends beyond the territory contained within its borders" (Program for Mexican Communities Abroad 1999). Zedillo's *völkisch* description of Mexican nationality is important because he stated the concept so explicitly in a high-profile document, but it continues the concept of *"el México de afuera"*[5] used by Presidents Echeverría and López Portillo (Gutiérrez 1986: 25).

The Mexican government's outreach to Mexicans in the United States also must be viewed in light of its attempt to create a pro-Mexican lobby akin to Jewish-American organizations that support Israeli interests in Washington (Santamaría Gómez 1994). In order to create a more politically powerful Mexican and Mexican-American community that still professes allegiance to Mexico, the Mexican Congress amended the Constitution in 1996 to enable Mexicans to hold dual nationality. Dual nationality allows Mexicans and children born abroad of Mexican parents to become citizens of other countries without losing the property rights of all Mexican citizens. A simple bureaucratic procedure at Mexican consulates allows naturalized U.S. citizens to retroactively assume dual Mexican and U.S. nationality. The law did not extend dual citizenship rights that would allow dual nationals to vote in Mexican elections (R. Smith 1998b).

The unintended consequence of the state's inclusive rhetoric, however, was to create a discursive breach (Foucault 1969) in the

---

[5] The community of Mexicans outside Mexico.

policies that excluded Mexican nationals in the United States from participation in Mexican electoral politics. Mexican citizens abroad do not have the full legal rights of citizenship—most conspicuously the right to vote from abroad. Mexicans in the United States began publicly appealing for the extension of suffrage to Mexicans living abroad, citing their continued Mexican identity and the remittances that fuel the Mexican economy. The PRI feared that Mexicans in the United States would tend to vote for the opposition, yet it could not openly reject extending suffrage without alienating the same migrants it was trying to co-opt (Rivera Salgado 1999, R. Smith 1998b). In debates in Congress and the Mexican media, non-migrants often challenged the rights of Mexicans in the United States to participate in Mexican politics. As a commentator wrote in a regional newspaper in Michoacán, "Some unhappy person, who was possibly brainwashed in a Yankee university, had the bad idea that Mexicans who renounce their fatherland and swear loyalty to the flag of the stars and stripes should not lose their Mexican nationality for this felony, but rather should keep intact the rights of citizenship" (Guerrero 1998). Guerrero concluded that dual nationals were not really Mexicans and that they would be a tool of the United States to "screw over" Mexico.

The interactions between the state and its nationals abroad offer a fascinating locus to study a social contract that is actually being negotiated rather than summoned from a mythical genesis, as Lockeian political philosophy would have it (Honig 1998). Very few citizens have much choice about their citizenship, but extra-territorial citizens are removed from the coercive apparatus of their home state. They are active partners in the citizenship contract. The motivations for individuals to demand citizenship and the motivations for states to extend citizenship become clearer by analyzing how states and transnational migrants attempt to draw the boundaries of extra-territorial citizenship.

The PRD, born out of the 1988 presidential campaign of Cuauhtémoc Cárdenas, has been the driving force behind the effort to extend suffrage to Mexicans abroad. Mexicans in California have helped the PRD by raising funds for campaign events in California, sending pro–PRD pamphlets to Mexico (some of which have been confiscated by Mexican authorities at the border), and, according to the PRI, illegally raising money for PRD candidates in Mexico (Pérez Godoy 1998). A group of PRD activists in Southern California, natives of Venustiano Carranza, Michoacán, say they send the Venustiano Carranza PRD office $365 every month for office expenses (author interview 2000). Larger cardenista groups have been institutionalized through organizations such as the Mexican Unity Group, the Mexican Assembly for Effective Suffrage, and the Organization of Mexicans for Democracy (OMD).[6] At the PRD's first national congress in Mexico City in 1990, the leader of the OMD and two Southern California cardenistas were appointed as California delegates to the PRD's national assembly (Martínez Saldaña 1993: 248–62). To the extent that cardenistas in California and Chicago work together with the PRD, and the PRD remains an official voice in the Mexican Congress for the right of Mexicans to vote abroad, the PRD is a transnational party (Pérez Godoy 1998: 16).

In July 1996, the Mexican Congress amended the 1917 Constitution to remove the clause that required Mexicans to vote for president in their district of residence in Mexico (Dillon 1998), though restrictions on voting for senators and deputies outside the district of residence remain. The amendment also paved the way for Mexicans living abroad to vote in Mexican presidential elections, but only if a secondary election law is passed that orders the Federal Electoral Institute (IFE) to organize elections outside the country (Molinar Horcasitas 1999). According to an IFE report issued in November 1998, the potential universe of Mexican citizens residing abroad on election day in July 2000 was an estimated 10.7 million people, 98 percent of whom were in the United States. The potential population of Mexican citizens residing abroad is roughly 14 percent of the total Mexican adult population. The definitional range of "citizen" extends from Mexican citizens in the United States who already hold a current Mexican voting credential (about 1.5 million persons) to naturalized citizens of other countries and adult children born abroad to Mexican parents. It is uncertain how many eligible voters would actually exercise their right if they could. According to the 1998 IFE study, of naturalized and unnaturalized Mexicans living in the United States, 65 percent said they knew there would be a presidential election in Mexico in 2000, and 83 percent said they wanted to vote in that election if they were able to do so in the United States. Fifty-five percent said they would vote if the process took less than an hour, and 21 percent said they would spend a day or more of their time to vote (Molinar Horcasitas 1999).

---

[6] Mexicans in the United States have also organized the less partisan Pro Vote Mexico 2000 Committee (Rivera Salgado 1999).

The PRI publicly accepts the principle of extending suffrage, but the contradictions in its position were revealed in a congressional vote on extending suffrage abroad that was forced by the opposition in July 1999. The enabling legislation passed the opposition-controlled Chamber of Deputies, but the PRI boycotted the session to consider the bill in the PRI–controlled Senate, thus effectively killing the measure (*La Jornada* 1999). The PRI based its arguments on technical objections, but it had clearly lost a discursive battle in its effort to exclude migrant voters who would likely tend to favor the center-left PRD or the center-right National Action Party (PAN).

Despite the failure of the vote abroad measure, candidates in the 2000 presidential election campaigned among Mexicans in the United States. PRI candidate Francisco Labastida refused to leave Mexico during the campaign, but his wife campaigned for him in Los Angeles. Cárdenas, again representing the PRD, campaigned in Los Angeles in May 2000. He urged Mexican voters living in California to travel to Mexico on election day and vote (J. Anderson 2000). The PAN has generally shown minimal interest in transnational migrant politics (Pérez Godoy 1998), but the party's Vicente Fox, the winning presidential candidate in 2000, campaigned in Chicago and California in May 2000. Before his presidential campaign, Fox was governor of Guanajuato, one of the top source states of U.S.–bound migrants. As governor, Fox established Casas Guanajuatenses in several U.S. cities to provide Guanajuatan migrants with legal aid under the My Community program (Sheridan 1998). Fox supports the right of Mexicans to vote abroad, and he publicly declared that migrants who sustain their hometowns' economies should exercise their influence with family members in Mexico. Fox told a crowd of hundreds of Mexicans and Chicanos in California's San Joaquin Valley, "We come to recommend that the best way to participate at this time is to phone your friends and family, to write letters, [or] to visit Mexico on July 2nd to vote." The Fox campaign distributed 500,000 pro-Fox postcards to Mexicans in the United States a month before the election and asked them to mail the cards to their families in Mexico. A Mexican industrialist sponsored the distribution of 20,000 telephone cards in the United States that he hoped Mexicans would use to call their friends and family at home to urge them to vote for Fox (J. Anderson 2000).

To accommodate Mexicans abroad who returned to Mexico to vote in the presidential election, the IFE established sixty-four special polling sites in Mexico's six border states. Each site was limited to 750 ballots, for a total of 48,000 ballots. Special polling sites are set up throughout Mexico to accommodate any Mexican citizen who is away from his district of residence on election day, but the number of special booths and ballots is strictly limited to avoid fraud. Unlike regular polling sites in which poll workers and party representatives match voters' identification cards with photographs of all registered voters in the precinct, special sites do not allow for such controls. The PRD and PAN, which would likely benefit most from increased numbers of special sites along the border, are wary of increasing the number of special ballots for fear of fraud. Individual migrants and some small caravans traveled from the United States to the special border sites, but according to press reports, the ballots quickly ran out on election day. Citizens in transit within Mexico outnumbered U.S.–based migrants at some of the border sites, thus diluting the impact of migrants at the ballot box (Fox 2000). Considering that 37.6 million ballots were cast for president (IFE 2000a), the migrant fraction of the 48,000 ballots cast in the frontier booths is negligible. Even if other migrants voted in their districts of residence or at scattered special booths in the interior, migrants' votes seem to have had little direct impact on the 2000 election.

Even if Mexican citizens were allowed to vote abroad in presidential elections, they could not vote in congressional elections without further changes in the law. Under Mexico's complicated system of congressional representation based on both single- and multiple-member districts, voters can only exercise a complete congressional vote in their district of residence. In 2000, PAN legislators introduced a bill to reserve ten seats in the 500–seat Chamber of Deputies for Mexicans living in the United States, although the measure's support among the PAN leadership is unclear and the vote abroad does not yet exist in any form (Sheridan 2000). PRD activists in California have distributed campaign posters calling for the election of deputies and senators from abroad in the 2003 midterm elections (author interview 2000). In fact, the creation of an extra-territorial electoral district is an established precedent elsewhere. The Colombian Constituent Assembly created a global extra-territorial district in 1991 to represent Colombians abroad (Guarnizo et al. 1999).

According to the Mexican Constitution, a candidate for deputy or senator must have been in "effective residence" in the state to be represented—or in a neighboring state—for at least six months before the election.[7] Yet several Mexicans who live at least part of the year in the United States ran for deputy in 2000. All three of the PRD candidates lost. Raúl Ross Pineda, an activist for the American Friends Service Committee who immigrated to Chicago in 1986, unsuccessfully campaigned in Illinois, Texas, California, and New York for a seat in Veracruz. Florencio Zaragoza, who splits his time between Tucson, Arizona, and Guaymas, Sonora, lost his bid to represent his Sonoran district. Los Angeles community organizer José Jacques Medina lost his bid as a candidate on the PRD's party list (Claiborne 2000, Steller 2000).

Curiously, the only successful candidate of the four ran for the PRI. Eddie Varón Levy, a 42-year-old Los Angeles legal consultant who has lived in the United States for over twenty years, was the fifth candidate on the PRI's party list in the Mexico City regional district. He is the first Mexican living abroad to win congressional office, but his election based on a party list can be attributed to his political connections within Mexico rather than to a base of support among Mexicans in the United States. Varón supports the right to vote abroad, however, and says he will represent Mexicans in the United States as well as in the Mexico City area (Olivo and Kraul 2000).

Basch, Glick Schiller, and Szanton-Blanc describe nation-building projects outside the state territory, such as the efforts of the Mexican government and political parties described above, as the construction of "deterritorialized nation-states" (1994). Smith and Guarnizo reject that term and use "trans-territorial nation-states" in its place. Sending states are expanding the borders of the national community they purport to protect. They are not eliminating territoriality as a basis of nationality (1998). The idea of a "deterritorialized nation-state" violates every constitutive element of a state in the Weberian definition of the body that has a monopoly on legitimate violence in a territory. Territoriality continues to define the state even as its citizens cross state borders. The state does not have any legitimate coercive power beyond its borders. As important as consulates are to the development of transnational practices, migrant affiliation with the consulates is largely voluntary. Even when the sending state attempts to persuade its citizens abroad without using violence, its activities are constrained by the receiving state. The legitimacy of the sending state's extra-territorial activities may not be recognized by its na-

---

[7] There are exceptions to this rule, but they do not include international migration.

tionals abroad. A deterritorialized nation, rather than a state, is already an established concept along the *völkisch* basis of German nationality (Brubaker 1992) or the collective national identities of diasporic populations (Clifford 1994). Recently, Glick Schiller has drawn the important distinction between the state and the nation, though it is not clear how it is then still possible to speak of a "transnational nation-state" (1999: 31). The concept of extraterritorial citizenship is useful because it allows us to explore the dynamic relationships between nations, states, territories, and individuals without conflating the nation and the state.

Migrants Working with the State: The Zacatecan Federation

Among the Mexican states, Zacatecas has the highest rate of U.S. migration per capita (Jones 1995: 51), though Michoacán sometimes claims this status as well (INEGI 1997: 18). Between 1 and 1.5 million Mexicans in the United States are of Zacatecan origin, and far more Zacatecans live in Los Angeles than in the Zacatecan state capital (Félix 1999a: 36). Zacatecans living in Los Angeles are organized into forty-three clubs that correspond to the migrants' respective sending communities. These clubs are affiliated with the Federation of Zacatecan Clubs, the oldest federation of hometown associations in Los Angeles. The Federation has developed a cadre of capable leaders and increased its effectiveness by encouraging a culture of participation and decentralization of power (Zabin and Escala Rabadán 1998).

The Federation has worked closely with the Zacatecan state government since 1985 when Governor Genaro Borrego visited Los Angeles. His visit led to the establishment of the Day of the Absent Zacatecans and the Program for Zacatecanos Abroad, in which the state government matched funds raised by HTAs to finance projects in their communities of origin (R. Smith 1998b: 34). The relationship was strengthened when the 2 X 1 Program was established under Governor Romo. Under 2 X 1, the federal and state governments each provided a matching dollar for every dollar raised by the Zacatecan Federation to finance public works projects (Goldring 1999: 6). The project was carried out on the federal level until 1996 (R. Smith 1998b: 37).

Under 2 X 1, only clubs registered with the Federation could participate. To Goldring, the program was presidentialist and *"gobernadorista"* given that the funds were not expended according to an agreed, specific budget. The program co-opted migrants into a clientelistic relationship with the Mexican state (Goldring 1999: 9). According to Smith, however, the funds for 2 X 1 usually were handled in the sending community by a committee of trusted friends of the Zacatecans in the United States. The committees could refuse to release the funds if they did not approve of the implementation of the projects, and delegations flew in from Los Angeles to monitor the project sites. "The absent Mexicans participated substantively in most steps of the decision-making and implementation of projects. The Secretary of Development set priorities regarding where matching funds would be spent but did not usually control the money the transmigrants remitted" (R. Smith 1998b: 35–37).

In 1993, Zacatecan migrant contributions were so high that the state government put a cap of $640,000 on its matching funds (Darling 1993). The following year, the entire contribution of the Federation, including matching funds, was $2 million.[8] During the 1990s, 200 projects were completed, including street paving; water, electrification, and light projects; and the construction of sports facilities (Félix 1999a: 37). In many communities, 2 X 1 funding was several times higher than regular official investment in public projects (Guarnizo 1998: 86–87, Goldring 1999: 9). The 2 X 1 program has since been replaced by Ramo 26, a much less participatory program which offers insights into the limits of government accountability to transnational migrants. Under the new program, the local municipal president has greater leeway to spend funds remitted from Zacatecans in the United States. "In practice the selection process is highly personalistic and often serves the political interests of the municipal president" (R. Smith 1998b: 37).

Attempts at corporatist control can backfire, however, especially when important actors operate outside the national boundaries of the state. In 1997, the PRI attempted to consolidate its control of the Zacatecan Federation in Los Angeles by forming a single confederation of the five Zacatecan federations in the United States, to be led by a president imposed by the consulate. However, the delegates changed the consulate's proposed charter for the Confederation and formally limited the influence of the consulate, the PACME, and the federal and state governments. The unintended consequence of the PRI's attempt to co-opt the movement was to promote the democratic process of debating a

---

[8] Annual remittances to Zacatecan migrant family members were $500 million during the same period (Guarnizo 1998: 86).

founding charter and freely electing Confederation leaders (R. Smith 1998b).

The 1998 gubernatorial election in Zacatecas offered a new opportunity for U.S.–based migrants to become heavily involved in Zacatecan state politics. Ricardo Monreal, a PRI defector who ran on the PRD ticket, made three trips to California during his campaign. Monreal praised the role of absent Zacatecans as agents of change in Zacatecas and ran radio ads in California asking Zacatecan migrants to call their relatives back home and encourage them to vote for him. Monreal's California campaign coordinator told the *Los Angeles Times* that "many people in California" who supported Monreal sent money to their families, who in turn contributed to the campaign. Zacatecan experts say that his courtship of migrant support was a significant, though not determining, factor in his victory (Sheridan 1998, R. Smith 1998b: 43).

Perhaps because he perceives a political debt to Zacatecans in the United States, Monreal has proposed that Zacatecans in Los Angeles directly elect two deputies to serve in the Zacatecas state legislature (Félix 1999a: 36–37). He also has proposed new regulations to make the administration of Ramo 26 more transparent and a plan to open a state Office of Migrant Affairs in Los Angeles to provide legal services to Zacatecan migrants. According to Smith, "if [Monreal] implements even some of these suggestions, it would take another step towards further institutionalizing the membership of transmigrants in the home society, and creating a transnational public sphere. The public contestation for the governorship of Zacatecas in California is an important step in incorporating the absent Zacatecans into the state's political community" (R. Smith 1998b: 44).

Hometown Associations and Public Projects: Local Forms of Citizenship

Many other transnational communities are organized around hometown associations. A tradition of such organizations lies in the mutual aid associations of migrants in Los Angeles in the early twentieth century (Escala Rabadán 1999). Most current associations have been formed within the last fifteen years, but at least one, the Club Ávalos of Chihuahua, dates back to 1958 (González Gutiérrez 1995: 69). Since 1990, the Program for Mexican Communities Abroad has aggressively supported the organization of HTAs, more than five hundred of which were registered with the

PACME in 1998. Membership figures for HTAs registered with the consulate in Los Angeles in 1995 reveal that there were approximately 150 HTAs with an average active membership of twenty-seven persons. Two-thirds of the clubs listed some form of sending community support as their principal project. Such projects included financing church repair, park construction, ambulances, potable water, school repair, clinic construction, drainage projects, sports facilities, libraries, wheel chairs, plaza remodeling, road paving, a fire truck, and a bull ring (R. Smith 1998b, González Gutiérrez 1995).

It is difficult to quantify how widespread these public projects are, but data collected in forty-eight communities with historically high emigration rates in west-central Mexico from 1990 to 1993 begin to give a rough approximation.[9] Table 1 shows that migrants helped finance at least one of eight different types of projects in one-third of the communities surveyed.

Table 1. Migrant Financing of Sending-Community Public Projects, 1990–1993

Projects That Migrants Helped Finance	Percent of Communities	Valid N
Electric service	7.3	41
Water service	12.0	41
Public lighting	10.0	40
Public market	3.5	29
Sports facilities	7.3	41
Churches	24.0	42
Schools	7.3	41
Plazas	17.0	36
Cases in Which Migrants Financed at Least One Project:	33.0	48

Data source: Mexican Migration Project 1996. COMCROSS. [MRDF] November 1996. Philadelphia: Population Studies Center, University of Pennsylvania [producer and distributor].

---

[9] These data are drawn from the Mexican Migration Project which compiled data from its own sending community surveys, statistical annuals, and Mexican censuses (Mexican Migration Project 1999).

The most common project, in which roughly a quarter of the communities received migrant assistance, was church building or repair. The survey did not ask about migrant financing of other projects that researchers have noted, such as paving roads, installing telephone service, or buying ambulances. A more complete consideration of other forms of migrant-financed projects would have yielded a higher number of communities where migrants have financed at least one project. All of the communities had historically high emigration rates, but they include a cross-section of urban, rural, indigenous, and mestizo communities. Larger samples of less aggregated data would be necessary in order to determine the kinds of communities where migrants tend to support public projects. Better data also would show the percentage of migrant financing in specific projects, though quantifying that number would be difficult because migrants sometimes remit a financial contribution while residents contribute their labor (R. Smith 1995, author interviews 1999).

In a study of migrant-household spending patterns in Zacatecas and Coahuila,[10] Jones found very low levels of expenditures on community projects. Among the Zacatecan and Coahuilan samples, three-tenths of one percent of migrant household expenditures was on community projects (Jones 1995). However, the survey may not have captured contributions made by U.S.–based migrants directly to community projects without the mediation of household members in the sending community.

Goldring's study of migration to the United States from Las Ánimas, Zacatecas, emphasizes transnational practices such as returning migrants' conspicuous consumption and migrant-sponsored community projects that migrants use to make status claims (1998). Higher wages and better job opportunities in the United States allow Animeños to return to Mexico and claim a higher class status through displays of wealth and cultural markers such as English language use. Goldring calls for a rethinking of analytical constructs such as "citizenship" and "nationality" as territoriality has become "unbound" from these constructs by transnational practices. But the kind of citizenship claimed by Animeño migrants in Las Ánimas is unclear. How can the concept of citizenship be applied to sending communities where a substantial portion of the population accepts migrants as sharing a

---

[10] In the Zacatecas study, 596 household surveys were conducted in Villanueva, Luis Moya, and Jerez. In the Coahuila study, 466 household surveys were conducted in Morelos and San Juan de Sabinas (Jones 1995).

community identity but denies them the full rights of community membership?

Robert Smith also questions categories such as "political community" and "citizenship." He suggests that neither the classical nor the post-national model of citizenship captures the demands for citizenship in the Mexican community of Ticuani[11] that are made by Ticuanis living in New York City. Ticuani represents a dramatic example of the potential political and economic power that U.S.–based migrants can develop in their sending communities. Half of the population of Ticuani now lives in New York City. The Ticuanis in New York have an extraordinarily well organized HTA called the Ticuani Solidarity Committee of New York, which mobilizes support for public works projects in Ticuani. The committee has successfully converted its economic power to fund such projects into a generally democratizing political influence.

The most important infrastructure project in which Ticuani migrants participated was a $150,000 project to provide water service for Ticuani. Through the committee, the migrants raised $100,000 in contributions of $300 or less. Rather than merely turning the money over to the municipal authorities, the committee actively took part in planning and supervising the project, to the point where committee leaders flew to Ticuani for the weekend for the express purpose of consulting with municipal authorities and contractors. When the project was completed, the New York committee asserted its power by controlling the water supply to each household in Ticuani. When residents of Ticuani wanted water service to their homes, they had to call their relatives in New York to pay the committee $300. Once the sum was paid, the committee would contact the municipality in Ticuani and the water would be turned on. The whole process was accompanied by stamps, seals, and other bureaucratic trappings, despite the fact that the committee was an unofficial group of private citizens.

The attempts of the New York migrants to use their public works contributions as a step to political power have been resisted by some municipal officials and have caused resentment within the town. Valid questions have been raised about the accountability of the committee itself, given that its members are not publicly elected officials. The municipal authorities would prefer that the New York migrants act as transnational tax collectors rather than political actors, while the New York migrants have sometimes tried to assert their power to the point that the New York commit-

---

[11] Ticuani is a pseudonym.

tee unsuccessfully ran a candidate for the municipal presidency who had not lived in Ticuani for more than thirty years (R. Smith 1995). The New York–based migrants and Ticuani residents also may have different conceptions of "progress." "The New Yorkers want to preserve the town's charm, and the locals want to modernize. The expatriates grew furious when some cobblestone streets were paved" (Sontag 1998: 10). This appears to be another example of the common observation that many migrants see their communities of origin as centers for vacation or retirement rather than production (Cornelius 1990: 80).

After several years of negotiations, Ticuanis in New York and Ticuani have agreed on the rough outlines of their political relationship. The municipal authorities realized they need the economic resources of the migrants and that the migrants' efforts and legitimacy as members of the community must be publicly recognized. The committee found that it must cooperate with the municipal authorities in order to initiate and administer projects effectively. Both sides have agreed that for an individual to compete as a candidate for municipal president, he or she must return to Ticuani and live there for at least one year before running for office. The interdependent political-economic relationship between the Ticuanis in New York and Ticuani seems to have created limits within which the boundaries of citizenship are negotiated.

Transnational Ethnic Politics

Unlike the mostly mestizo migrants from states like Zacatecas, Michoacán, and Jalisco, most Oaxacan migrants to California are indigenous Mixtecs, Zapotecs, or Triques. Indigenous ethnicity is often the basis for political organization in the United States that partially reproduces indigenous political systems from the sending communities. In many of the sending communities, the civil-religious *cargo* system is very much alive. Political power is achieved through the fulfillment of obligations—or cargos—that might include sponsoring a religious fiesta or serving as a local official. In carrying out these works, the individual earns social prestige that can be transformed into political power. All able-bodied males are also expected to participate in the *tequio* tradition of collective labor (Rivera Salgado 1999). Unlike in mestizo areas where such participation is relatively voluntary, in some indigenous communities nonparticipants are actually jailed.[12]

---

[12] Personal communication with Gaspar Rivera Salgado.

The cargo tradition is so strong that many absent migrants are elected to fill positions. If migrants wish to continue claiming membership in their community of origin, they must return to fulfill their obligation. In some areas of mass emigration, the cargo system has changed. Long cargos of more than a year are becoming less common, because asking someone to drop out of the migratory stream for an extended period would be financially devastating and hence reduce the number of people willing to fill the cargos (Woodman Colby 1998: 101). The migration of large numbers of men also has left a shortage of eligible cargo holders. Some communities have allowed women to take on religious cargos for the first time, although the inclusion of women has been vigorously resisted in other communities (Woodman Colby 1998: 95, Iszaevich 1988: 193–94). In other areas, the entire cargo system is in decline, partially as a result of massive out-migration, and even migrants who return from the United States to fill their cargos have ambiguous feelings about the heavy economic burden (Rivera Salgado 1999).

Oaxacan migrant leaders in California have tried to strengthen ties between migrants and their communities of origin by organizing hometown associations. They have done this very successfully, despite the fact that, unlike many mestizo migrant networks with between sixty and one hundred years of migration history, the Oaxacan networks typically were formed no earlier than the 1960s (Rivera Salgado 1999). Oaxacan migrants also tend to be much more geographically dispersed in the United States than mestizo migrant populations such as the Zacatecans (R. Smith 1998b: 49). Some of the Oaxacan migrant organizations foster a strong sense of ethnic identity. Although ethnicity may not have been the basis of self-identification in Mexico, it becomes an essential building block for grassroots transnational mobilizing in the United States (Nagengast and Kearney 1990: 62).[13] The interests of some of these associations extend beyond the milieu of individual sending communities to include regional and national-level concerns. Organizations such as the 2,000–member Binational Indigenous Oaxacan Front (FIOB) are truly transnational, with offices in California, Oaxaca, and areas of internal migration such as Baja California (Rivera Salgado 1999).

---

[13] Of course, this does not suggest a monolithic ethnic self-identification of indigenous migrants. Woodman Colby found that most Mixtec migrants she met in the United States did not identify themselves as Mixtecs (1998: 211–12).

A 1997 protest dramatized the Oaxacans' transnational mobilizing capability and their broad agenda. A group of Oaxacan migrant farmworkers held a demonstration in front of the Mexican consulate in Fresno, California, to press their demands for the Mexican federal government to recognize the San Andrés peace accords signed with the Zapatista Army of National Liberation (EZLN) in 1996. Protesters simultaneously held a press conference in Tijuana and led a caravan from the Oaxacan town of Juxtlahuaca to Oaxaca City. In 1996, the FIOB participated in the Zapatista-sponsored Indigenous National Congress in San Cristóbal de las Casas, Chiapas. The congress selected the FIOB to serve as the official liaison between the congress and indigenous migrants in the United States. Oaxacans living in the United States also participated in the *"consulta"* that the Zapatistas carried out in March 1999 to publicize their demands for indigenous rights in Mexico. The FIOB coordinated the consulta in California with other human rights organizations and regional Californian PRD committees (Rivera Salgado 1999). According to FIOB leader Rufino Domínguez, "Oaxacan immigrants also have the political right to decide what happens in our country [Mexico], and we hope that in Mexico they will also think about those of us who emigrate, because here we face many injustices" (in B. Rodríguez 1999, my translation).

As Goldring has noted, migrants sometimes have had to leave their country in order to increase their political influence within it (Goldring 1996: 88). Physically removed from the repressive forces of the state, Oaxacan migrants have been able to agitate loudly for human rights reform in Mexico. Mexican consular officials privately admit they want to avoid the negative publicity generated by Oaxacan protests in the United States. This gives migrant organizations an opening to apply political leverage. As a migrant leader explained, "If something happens in Oaxaca, we can put protesters in front of the consulates in Fresno, Los Angeles, Madera" (R. Smith 1998b).

Oaxacans in California have effectively used their own media such as Fresno-based Radio Bilingüe to pressure U.S. and Mexican officials on human rights abuses in Mexico. In October 1997, masked men kidnapped seven indigenous organization leaders in Oaxaca. Radio Bilingüe broadcast appeals for their release, and Oaxacan migrant leaders in Fresno made similar demands in a meeting with Oaxacan state officials. The kidnapped men ultimately were released, reportedly in part because of the mobilization of human rights organizations on both sides of the border (R.

Smith 1998b). Clearly, the fact that the Mexican government is pursuing a policy of alignment with the United States is partially framing the democratic possibilities exercised by grassroots migrant organizations. The migrant organizations have been able to capitalize on those circumstances and further pressure for a Mexican democracy that accepts indigenous political actors and respects the human rights of its citizens.

Oaxacan migrants in the United States are participating in the political life of Mexico, from small local development projects to involvement with national congresses. The migratory experience itself and the indigenous political-cultural milieu from which it arose have contributed to the development of strong organizations. Because the political activity of a group like the FIOB is so broad, it is more difficult to measure the precise effects that may be attributable to its actions than if it were exclusively involved in community politics. The FIOB is one of many organizations in Mexico and around the world that are trying to influence the conflict in Chiapas. However, the institutionalization of a range of organizations across the indigenous migrant movement suggests that Oaxacan migrants will continue to push a transnational political agenda.

Activism or Apathy? Migration's Political Impacts on Sending Communities

The micro-level political effects of migration on Mexican sending communities have been the subject of surprisingly little research. During his investigation in the 1920s, Mexican anthropologist Manuel Gamio hypothesized that return migrants were the root of the labor union movement, the agrarian reform, and the Mexican Revolution (Gamio 1969). The Mexican mutual aid organizations in Los Angeles particularly impressed him.

> Such a well-developed spirit of sociability, fraternalism, and mutual aid undoubtedly contributes much to the well-being and progress of the immigrants. Indirectly its beneficent influence, transmitted to Mexico through the repatriated immigrants, is of great importance there. It helps to modify the isolation of individuals in the country and small towns; it awakes the desire for social co-operation; it disciplines the character and the labor of the workman; and in general, it stimulates many useful activities (Gamio 1969: 135–36).

Discussing research conducted seventy years after Gamio's work, Mexican political scientist and commentator Jorge Castañeda made a hopeful prediction about the democratizing effects of return migrants.

> The type of political activity that is emerging among cardenistas in California—be it in Los Angeles, San Jose, or Fresno—will most likely be brought home to Mexico through the migrants themselves. And inevitably, practices such as fund-raising, voter registration drives, access to the local media, freewheeling, often divisive debate—all forms of political endeavor largely absent from Mexico and unprecedented in the migrants' small towns and villages—will blossom in Mexico.... Where the migrants make a fundamental difference is in breaking down obstacles and resistance to change in their native towns and villages (Castañeda 1993: 40).

Is there historical evidence to support Gamio's and Castañeda's assertion of migrants' political relationships with their communities of origin, much less that migrants have a democratizing influence? While Gamio's evidence is thin in many respects, there is substantial evidence from other sources that migrants sometimes return with changed expectations toward government that have important consequences at the local level. Changed expectations often relate to expanded conceptions of rights to government services. The municipal president of Jerez, Zacatecas, is facing a generational problem as migrants who left in the 1950s and 1960s are returning and demanding health services that Jerez has never had (Félix 1999b: 37). In Copándaro, Michoacán, returning migrants have lobbied for enlarging the local telephone network. They speak of the need to pave the streets, resurface the highway, and automate water service. According to Rionda Ramírez, "Cultural change manifests itself in two ways: attitudinal and physical change. The first is found at the individual level, with an increase in expectations and the ambition for betterment; the second is felt in the accelerated physical change of the town" (1992: 261, my translation).

In a "culture of outmigration" (Cornelius 1990: 77) or "northernization" (Alarcón 1988: 338), the life of a sending community becomes so linked to out-migration that even when migrants return for brief periods, they frequently are apathetic toward the well-being of the community. Their productive interests are focused on the United States. Such apathy has important implications for nonparticipation in community politics. In Tlazazalca, Michoacán, for example, there is a general disregard for the political process because residents are so connected to life in the North. According to one author, this disengagement has retarded any local opposition and enabled the PRI to maintain its hegemony (Hernández Santiago 1985: 67–68).

In the Bajío of Michoacán, a tendency for migrants to be absent year-round, the migration of whole families, the reduced frequency and duration of return trips to sending communities, and a focus on housing and business in the United States have weakened the political culture of the *ejidos*.[14] "The younger migrant generation lacks information about and shows a certain apathy toward ejido resources in the home village." Young people especially are disinterested in agriculture. The importance of the ejido vis-à-vis other local political structures has thus been weakened (Zendejas Romero 1998, quote p. 181).

Large-scale, sustained migration from Tlacuitapa, Jalisco, has concentrated ejido land among a small economic and political elite. The extended absences of migrant ejidatarios enabled corrupt local authorities to sell communal land illegally for personal profit. Absent migrants faced the threat of having their land confiscated under the laws of the Agrarian Reform and therefore had an increased incentive to illegally sell or rent their ejidatario rights. Even though reforms to Article 27 now allow absentee land ownership, the younger generation in particular does not see farming as a viable economic enterprise and is likely to abandon the land (Cornelius 1998a: 234–44). In a survey conducted in 1988 and 1989, 79.5 percent of interviewees felt that emigration was required to get ahead in life (Cornelius 1990: 78).

> Migration to the United States becomes a complete substitute for local economic activity—a solution to one's economic problems that is considerably easier and less risky than starting a business in the home community, or investing in agricultural infrastructure, or organizing a production cooperative. It is also difficult to become concerned about the lack of public services, unpaved roads, or other deficiencies of the home

---

[14] *Ejidos* were inalienable, communally held lands until 1991, when the Agrarian Reform detailed in Article 27 of the 1917 Constitution was amended (Cornelius and Myhre 1998).

> community, when one spends most of his time in the
> United States; so there is little civic spirit, and no col-
> lective efforts to secure public goods (p. 77).

In the Oaxacan village of San Sebastián Nicananduta, interest in the cargo system of civil-religious community leadership positions is declining, in part because it is impossible to hold cargos and migrate simultaneously (Woodman Colby 1998: 94). Migration has been blamed for a similar weakening of the *faena* tradition of collective labor for community projects in indigenous Purépecha regions of Michoacán, which has lessened the pool of available laborers and contributed to a monetarization of the economy. Dinerman found that community buildings in Huecorio were in disrepair because faena labor no longer maintained them, although a faena in the form of $10 contributions was being resurrected among Huecorians in Los Angeles (Dinerman 1982: 72).

As the examples from Zacatecas, Oaxaca, and Puebla show, some transnational migrants may continue to find ways to become politically involved in their sending communities, but for every transnational activist, how many migrants—or even non-migrants—have become disengaged from politics? Migration may cause migrants to become disengaged from the politics of their sending communities, and it may cause non-migrants to become disengaged as well by providing an easier alternative than working for local change. Even when migrants organize transnationally, political apathy may increase in the sending community among non-migrants who expect migrants to finance and lead community development (Glick Schiller and Fouron 1999). The relationship between the practice of citizenship and transnational migration can only be fully understood through in-depth case studies.

CHAPTER 4

Sahuayo, Michoacán, and Its "Colonies"

Site Selection and Methods

Most empirical evidence dealing with Mexican transnational migrants is drawn from the experience of migrants in highly organized associations. The examples in the studies discussed in chapter 3 appear to be the exception to the experience of most Mexican migrants, who are not involved in institutionalized transnational politics. While such rarefied instances of migrant organizing are crucial to an understanding of the potential strength of transnational migrant political action, it would be misleading to assume their relevance to the daily experience of the majority of Mexican migrants. By focusing on the participation of migrants who organize along more informal networks, one can gain a broader understanding of the range of alternative paradigms.

Michoacano migration is a fruitful area for exploration of less-institutionalized associations. Michoacán has been one of the biggest source states of migrants to the United States for the last century (Massey et al. 1987, Ochoa Serrano 1998). In 1992, Michoacán had the highest rate of international migration of any state in Mexico (INEGI 1997: 18). There are an estimated 1.4 million documented Michoacanos and 700,000 undocumented Michoacanos in the United States, whose family remittances of more than US$600 million a year equaled Michoacán's state budget for 1996 (Gurza 1998, Robles et al. 1997).

In Los Angeles and Orange County, Michoacán is the second highest source state of migrants, yet Michoacanos are far less organized than populations of migrants such as the Zacatecans or Jaliscienses who share similar long histories of migration to California. In fact, Michoacanos are much more organized in Chicago than they are in Los Angeles, despite their smaller population in Chicago (Goldring 1999: 12). There are fourteen hometown associations among the estimated 200,000 Michoacanos in the Chicago area (Espinosa 1999), while there are eleven HTAs among the es-

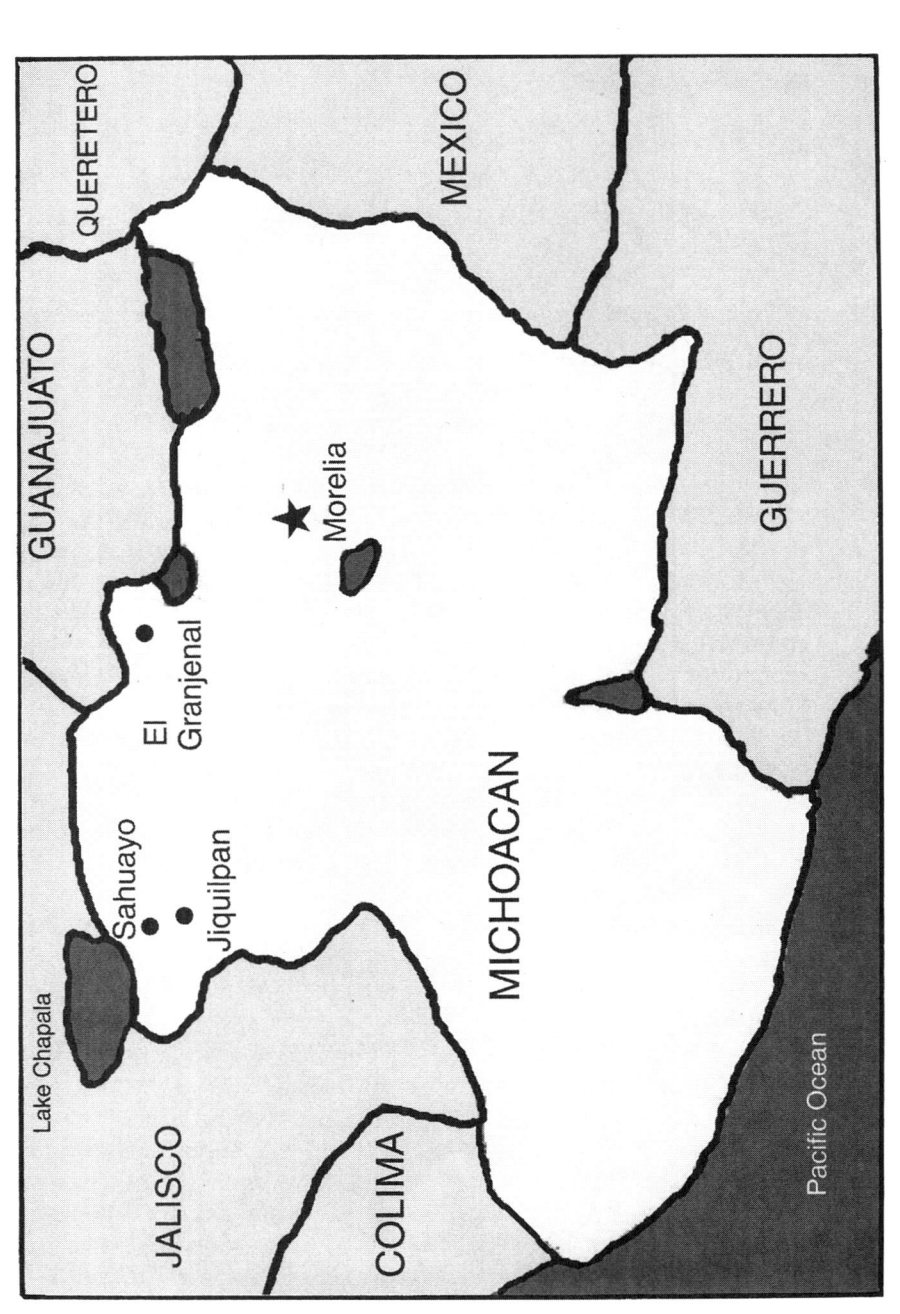

Figure 1. Primary research sites in Michoacán

timated 261,000 Michoacanos in Los Angeles (Zabin and Escala Rabadán 1998).[15] The important difference is the organization of the Chicago HTAs into an active federation.

Michoacano HTAs created the Federation of Michoacano Clubs in Illinois in 1997 at the urging of the Mexican consulate, which used the Zacatecan federation as its model. Michoacán Governor Víctor Manuel Tinoco Rubí has visited Michoacanos in Chicago three times, made at least one visit to Los Angeles, and is actively trying to encourage Michoacanos in Los Angeles and northern Illinois to invest in their sending communities. From 1996 to 1999, Michoacanos in the United States worked with the state government to fund more than one hundred projects (Walker 1999). However, these projects are organized on an ad hoc basis, and there is only a weak institutional framework in place for their development (author interviews 1999). While it is not clear how much oversight the migrants really exercise, the fact that the political discourse recognizes U.S.–based migrants as legitimate members of their sending communities is significant in itself. Four of the clubs alone—from San Miguel Epejan, Ciudad Hidalgo, La Purísima, and La Luz—have contributed a total of $650,000 to their communities of origin (Espinosa 1999).

Michoacán is also an interesting site to explore the relationships between migrants and the Mexican state because Michoacán is a hotbed of opposition politics (Bruhn 1999). Jorge Zepeda Patterson explains that migration could be considered an escape valve for political dissent, but Michoacán's history:

> abounds in cases of leaders and social activists who, when migrants, became conscious of their rights and the possibilities of defending them. The many cases of municipal conflicts in the 1980s are replete with examples of conflicts led by this type of person. Only direct investigation can clarify the relationship that surely exists between migratory phenomena and local political processes (Zepeda Patterson 1990, my translation).

---

[15] In general, the size of the population from a particular Mexican state is not a strong predictor of the level of organization. Large populations of Guanajuatenses, Duranguenses, Baja Californianos, and Capitalinos (from Mexico City) are relatively unorganized. HTAs are mostly organized around small towns and rural communities. Guadalajara is the source of more migrants in Los Angeles than any other city in Mexico, but there is no Guadalajaran HTA in Los Angeles (González Gutiérrez 1995).

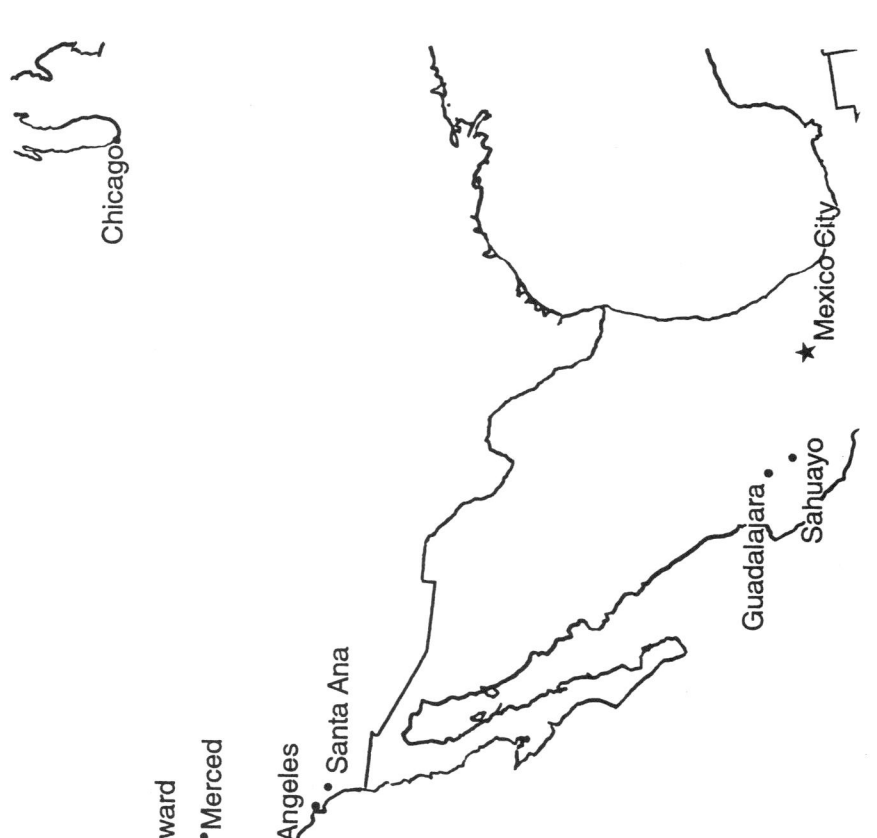

Figure 2. Sahuayo, Michoacán, and its satellites

I chose a research site with a large concentration of Michoacanos as the study's point of departure. Santa Ana, California, a city of 300,000 inhabitants, is located 50 kilometers south of Los Angeles in Orange County. So many Michoacanos live in Santa Ana that they affectionately call it "Santa Ana, Mich." Sixty-five percent of the population of Santa Ana is Latino, and 92 percent of the Latino population is of Mexican origin (*Hispanic Databook* 1994). Among Michoacanos, the population of Sahuayan origin is particularly large. Sahuayans have verbally appropriated the space by calling Santa Ana "*Sahuayito*" or "*Sahuayo Chiquito*" (Little Sahuayo). As one Sahuayan who has lived in both cities put it, "Santa Ana and Sahuayo are the same—same people, same barrio."

Most academic studies of Mexican communities with high emigration rates concentrate on small towns and villages (Roberts et al. 1999). In contrast, Sahuayo has 60,000 inhabitants as measured in the 1995 INEGI census, and twice that many according to the municipal government (*Plan de Desarrollo* 1999) (table 2).[16] Mexican migrants to the United States are increasingly of urban origin (Marcelli and Cornelius n.d.), suggesting that migration studies almost exclusively carried out in villages and rural communities are no longer adequate. Sahuayo offers the methodological advantages of an urban site with a long history of mass migration.

The fieldwork for the study was conducted from June 1999 to July 2000 in Santa Ana, Inglewood, and Los Angeles, California. I spent July and August 1999 in Michoacán and made visits there in December 1999 and July 2000. Sahuayo was the primary research site in Michoacán. I conducted seventy-five semi-structured interviews, as well as many informal conversations, in Spanish. Informants in Sahuayo included the last two PRI, PAN, and PRD candidates, respectively, for the municipal presidency; the current presidents of the parties' municipal committees; current and former leaders of Sahuayan migrant networks in Santa Ana, Los Angeles, Merced, and Chicago; Catholic priests; leaders of civic associations; journalists; and current and former migrants whom I contacted using snowball sampling with diverse points of entry. Interviews in California were conducted with Sahuayan community leaders, priests, and other migrants. The universe of inter-

---

[16] The municipal president alleges that the federal government deliberately undercounts the population in order to minimize its expenditures, which are calculated on a per capita basis.

viewed migrants was largely restricted to those currently or formerly active in transnational public activities. Most informants were men between the ages of 30 and 65, because these are the individuals who tend to be the most active participants in the public activities that are the subject of the study.

Table 2. Municipio of Sahuayo, Michoacán, 1995

Demographics	
Population	60,000
Percent of municipio living in city of Sahuayo[1]	94
Percent of males in the population	47.9
Annual percentage rate of population increase, 1990–1995	1.9
Percent population < 15 yrs	36
Literate percent of population >15 yrs	86
Percent population >5 yrs who speak an indigenous language	0.09
Housing	
Percent of houses with electricity	97.6
Percent of housing with plumbing	92.7
Median occupants per housing unit	4.8
Municipio Expenditures[2]	
Public works (pesos)	1,494,882
Total (pesos)	13,764,541
Geography	
Size	128 km^2
Elevation	1500 m

[1] 1990
[2] 1996
Sources: INEGI 1991, 1997, 1998; *Plan de Desarrollo Municipal* 1999.

In order to compare the experience of Sahuayo with other Michoacano towns, I interviewed municipal presidents in the three neighboring *municipios*[17] of Cojumatlán, Venustiano Carranza, and Jiquilpan. Municipal officials, local elites, and migrant

---

[17] A *municipio* is roughly equivalent to a county in the United States.

club leaders from Jiquilpan were interviewed in Jiquilpan and Inglewood. I also visited El Granjenal in the municipio of Puruándiro. El Granjenal is of particular interest because there are many more people from El Granjenal in Santa Ana than in El Granjenal. Community leaders were interviewed in the indigenous Purépecha town of Tarejero in the municipio of Zacapu, and other informal conversations were held with *jefes de tenencia*[18] and former migrants in Purépecha towns around Lake Pátzcuaro.

The interviews were driven by the following questions, with particular attention paid to differences between the responses of current migrants and political elites in Sahuayo.

- What are the forms of migrants' collective transnational participation in the public life of the town?
- What motivates these collective practices?
- Are these practices political or potentially political?
- What are the discourses of rights and obligations for migrants in the public life of the town?
- What is the relationship between these discourses and practices of citizenship?

Sahuayo, Michoacán, and Its Migrants

Sahuayo rises on a hillside 15 kilometers southeast of Mexico's largest lake—Chapala. A century ago the lake reached Sahuayo, but over the years the shoreline has receded, extending a swath of fertile farmland called the Ciénega of Chapala. Some of the first international emigrants from the region began their trip north by steamship across Lake Chapala to Guadalajara, 125 kilometers to the northwest (Ochoa Serrano 1998), but today it is only an hour and a half by car from Sahuayo to the Guadalajara airport and a three-hour flight from there to Southern California. Alternately, a Sahuayan bus company offers daily departures and US$85 one-way fares to two destinations on the California border—Mexicali and Tijuana.

I arrived in Sahuayo on a bus, several hours after the overnight flight from Los Angeles landed in Guadalajara. My wife and I were standing on a street corner finding our bearings when a man in his twenties approached and offered us a ride. Luis Manuel had

---

[18] A *jefe de tenencia* is the mayor of a small town.

just arrived from Compton, near Los Angeles, where he had lived for the past eleven years. As he maneuvered his mini-van down Sahuayo's main street, we joked about how traffic in Sahuayo was worse than in Los Angeles. Like the van, at least a quarter of the cars had license plates from California, Illinois, and other U.S. states. Shoppers bustled in every imaginable kind of retail shop and strolled past travel agency windows posting the lowest fares to Los Angeles and Chicago. Every few blocks, there was an automated teller machine behind gleaming glass or Mexican and American flags advertising a *casa de cambio* (exchange house). This was not the economically depressed community one might expect to find in an area of such high emigration. Luis Manuel dropped us off in the plaza and gave us his telephone number, urging us to call him if we needed anything. I wondered how he was received by strangers on his first day in Compton.

Not surprisingly, the plaza is the center of Sahuayo's social life. An arcade around its fountain and wooden kiosk dates to 1910. During the day, straw-hatted men who are almost as old as the arcade stake out their turf in one corner of the plaza. Rubén, age 74, swam the Rio Grande in 1946 to pick grapefruit in Pecos, Texas, with dozens of other Sahuayans before returning to the United States twice as a bracero. Now he sells snacks and newspapers to pedestrians. On Sunday evenings, hundreds of Sahuayans gather to hear free concerts sponsored by the city hall. A statue of Miguel Hidalgo shakes a fist toward young elites in fashionable clothes who lounge on the steps outside a nightclub, watching their friends speed past on mopeds. Pickup trucks cruise past, blaring *rock-en-español*, *banda*, or Kenny G. Behind the plaza, the illuminated twin spires of the cathedral "soar like white doves," in the words of "Sahuayo, Mi Tierra," a song I first heard in Santa Ana.

Sahuayo has been the source of sustained emigration to the United States for almost a century, despite its position as the economic capital of the Ciénega for even longer. Its economic strength in the region stems largely from its strategic positioning on the old road between Mexico City and Guadalajara (González 1979). Sahuayo has much stronger social and economic links to Guadalajara than to the Michoacán state capital of Morelia 210 kilometers to the east. Throughout the 1700s, the giant hacienda of Guaracha absorbed the available land around Sahuayo, reducing Sahuayo's opportunities for agricultural production and leading to a focus on commerce and artisan production in its stead. Sandal manufacture dates back to the mid–1800s in Sahuayo (Forbes Adams 1984). By

1990, Sahuayo produced 2 million pairs of sandals (*guaraches*) a year. The industry supports an estimated one in four Sahuayans; these artisans work in scores of small workshops and homes (Zepeda Patterson 1990: 153).

Sahuayo's relationship to agriculture today is primarily in the sale of agricultural inputs and, to a lesser extent, in the sale of agricultural products. By the mid–1980s, Sahuayo was attracting customers from throughout northwest Michoacán and southeast Jalisco. Among the primary goods sold were animal fodder, wholesale grains, furniture, groceries, pharmaceuticals, shoes, and electric goods. Small factories made ceramic tiles, clothing, and shoes (Forbes Adams 1994). Sahuayo was once famed for its sombrero production as well, but this industry is declining. To this day, there are no large factories in any sector, even in the thriving sandal industry.

The economic and political history of the region in the early twentieth century continues to reverberate in Sahuayan politics. During the Cristero War in the 1920s, in which Catholic rebels fought the central government and the Agrarian Reform, Sahuayo was an important regional base for the Cristeros (González 1979). Conservative Catholicism and anti-*cardenismo* continued to reinforce each other as Lázaro Cárdenas's Agrarian Reform expropriated local haciendas and ranches (Vargas González 1993). A strong rivalry grew between Sahuayo and its smaller but more politically powerful neighbor, Jiquilpan, 10 kilometers to the south. Jiquilpan was the hometown and political base of Lázaro Cárdenas and his brother, Dámaso, who dominated Ciénega politics for more than thirty years (Ochoa Serrano 1999, Zepeda Patterson 1989).

The Church throughout Michoacán, but especially in the Ciénega, has sought to keep the population immune from cardenismo. While the Church does not attempt to assume direct political power, it is an extremely influential pressure group (Zepeda Patterson 1990: 76). Sahuayo is still known throughout the region as a bastion of Catholicism and opposition to the secular state (Forbes Adams 1994, González 1979, author interviews 1999). As in many Michoacano communities, social life revolves around religious festivals, and priests are among the most important community leaders. The Church also penetrates civil society through its hospitals and charity organizations (Zepeda Patterson 1990, author interviews 1999).

The direct exercise of political power in Sahuayo historically has been restricted to a business elite whose interests have been served regardless of the party in office. From 1963 to 1986, every municipal president, with one exception, was a businessman. The PAN has been a strong presence in Sahuayo since the 1940s, and it was able to elect a municipal president in 1962, one of the earliest PAN municipal victories in the entire country. A coalition elected PAN candidate Salvador Múgica Manzo after the PRI candidate openly confronted the Church over control of a secondary school. However, the 1962 election was considered less a sign of *panista* strength than evidence of the power of the Church. The election did not threaten the PRI, which soon co-opted Múgica Manzo (Vargas González 1993).

The PAN lay relatively dormant in Sahuayo until the early 1980s, when the Sahuayan commercial class perceived that Michoacán's governor, Cuauhtémoc Cárdenas, was threatening its interests (Vargas González 1993). Over the last fifteen years, the PAN and PRI have alternated power in Sahuayo. Two panistas have been elected municipal president in this period, though the current municipal president is a *priísta*. The PRD has never won a municipal election, though it runs candidates in major elections. Sahuayo's historical antagonism with cardenismo and the wide-spread perception in Sahuayo that the PRD is an agent of secularism and even atheism have limited the PRD's success. The opposition Green Party of Mexico (PVEM) ran a candidate in the 1998 municipal elections, although the party has little support and is rumored to have been financed by the PRI to split the opposition vote. The PVEM candidate left to live in Orange County following the election.

Sahuayo has extremely high rates of emigration and has been a source of migrants to the North[19] for at least eighty years. It was impossible to find a single person who did not have at least one close family member in the United States. The majority of men questioned had been to the North at least once. Most Sahuayans who were interviewed perceived that the rate of female migration also is increasing, a finding in line with survey research elsewhere in west-central Mexican communities with high migration rates (Massey et al. 1994: 1512, Durand 1994: 157). Despite Sahuayo's active commercial life, there are not enough well-paying jobs to keep Sahuayans from migrating to the United States and cities like Guadalajara and Mexico City. The culture of migration is so strong

---

[19] In Michoacán, *el Norte* refers to the United States, and migrants living in the United States are called *norteños*. While norteño is not considered a derogatory term by most migrants and non-migrants, I met one long-term migrant who disliked the term because he said it suggested he was "less Sahuayan."

that even children express a desire to go to the United States, at least to experience the adventure. Educators complain that their students do not apply themselves in their studies because they expect to leave as soon as they become adults.

The first ten Sahuayan migrants to the United States went to Galveston, Texas, and Chicago in 1917. Contracted braceros began arriving in Santa Ana in the 1940s (author interviews with surviving family members 1999). Today there are four large concentrations of Sahuayans in California. After Santa Ana, the largest populations are in Los Angeles, Merced, and Hayward. There is also a concentration of Sahuayans in Chicago and northern Indiana.

The population of Sahuayans living in Santa Ana is difficult to estimate.[20] The number of residents of Mexican origin is only measured in the decennial U.S. census which typically undercounts immigrants, especially the undocumented (*Binational Study* 1997). Data about hometown origin are only available from self-reporting to the Mexican consulate. Despite the limitations of the data, an estimate can be made using 1996 voluntary registration data from the Mexican consulate in Santa Ana and the 1990 U.S. census.[21] Twenty percent of Orange County residents—480,000 people—described themselves as Mexican-origin in 1990 (*Hispanic Databook* 1994). Approximately 43,000 Mexican nationals registered with the consulate in 1996. Using the 1990 census figures for the Mexican population, we can conservatively estimate that approximately one of eleven Mexican-origin residents was registered with the consulate in 1996. Three of the five Mexican cities most represented in the consulate register are in Michoacán—Jiquilpan, Sahuayo, and Morelia. The register lists 287 Jiquilpenses and 283 Sahuayans. It is impossible to know how registration rates vary by town of origin, but if we assume that Sahuayans follow the average registration rate, we can estimate a 1996 population of roughly 3,000 Sahuayans in Orange County.

Ample evidence from interviews suggests that the vast majority of Sahuayans in Orange County live in Santa Ana. Sahuayans live throughout the city and are not especially concentrated in any neighborhood. Neither are Sahuayans concentrated in any eco-

---

[20] I do not have access to consular data from other cities in the United States with high concentrations of Sahuayans. Sahuayan municipal officials do not know how many Sahuayans live in the United States.

[21] This method is derived from Zabin and Escala Rabadán's calculation of the number of Mexicans in Los Angeles by state of origin (1998).

nomic niche. Most are blue-collar workers, but a number own restaurants and small businesses. There are no reliable data on the proportion of Sahuayans living in Santa Ana or elsewhere in the United States who have legal status, but interview data and the estimates of migrants suggest that neither legal nor illegal status is overwhelmingly dominant.

The municipio of Sahuayo estimates that 50 percent of Sahuayan families receive remittances from family members in the United States (*Plan de Desarrollo* 1999). The circulation of dollars in the economy is impressive. In 1999, there were eighteen casas de cambio. The owner of four of the casas estimated that he exchanges an average of over $100,000 a day, including cashing U.S. money orders, U.S. pension checks, and exchanging cash. It is impossible to know what portion of these dollars is from remittances and what portion is due to the use of dollars as a common currency in Mexico for large transactions, but the importance of remittances as an economic pillar of Sahuayo is unquestioned.

Remittances in Sahuayo are typically used for personal consumption or housing construction, as researchers have found elsewhere in Mexican communities with high rates of emigration (Massey et al. 1987). Housing construction and furnishings provide a sustained source of employment in Sahuayo. For example, the owner of a chain of four hardware stores with forty years in business estimated that 40 percent of his sales are to norteños. A carpenter who employs ten men in his workshop said that most of his business is with norteños, who pay top prices for custom furniture and fittings. The U.S.–based migrant portion of their businesses has increased in the last ten years, unlike the decrease in migrant investment in housing and furnishings found in other high-emigration communities as many migrants settle in the United States (Cornelius 1998a).

Sahuayan businessmen and political leaders agree that only a small share of remittances is directly invested in businesses. Still, there is survey and anecdotal evidence that suggests that many small businesses in Sahuayo are started at least in part with capital earned by migrants who worked in the North and then returned to settle in Sahuayo. In her study of sandal production in the 1980s, Forbes Adams found that between 1950 and 1985, 6.2 percent of sandal workshops and 11.7 percent of subcontractor sandal workshops were formed primarily with capital saved from migration (1984). In 1999, I found a variety of businesses started with earnings from the North, such as clothing stores, restaurants, an agricultural seed store, a sporting goods store, a printing business, and an avocado distributorship. Entrepreneurial former migrants may themselves underestimate the influence of migrant investment by neglecting to consider indirect investment mechanisms. For example, one businessman said that he did not start his beverage distribution franchise with capital he raised as a wage laborer in the United States. Yet he went on to describe how he used his savings to buy two pieces of property in Sahuayo. Upon returning from Chicago, he built a house on one property and sold the other to raise the capital to start his business.

Migration is also an emergency debt-relief strategy that enables entrepreneurs to bail themselves out in hard times. For example, a sandal workshop owner went bankrupt in the 1980s economic crisis. He went to work in Chicago and saved enough money to pay off his debts in Sahuayo. When he returned, he was able to obtain a loan with his clean credit and start a new workshop that today employs sixty workers (author interview 1999). Forbes Adams found that the same emergency strategy was used by sandal makers in the 1970s (1984).

"We are like ants who go out and bring food back home," explained a Sahuayan who worked as a merchant in Mexico City for ten years before returning to build a two-story home in Sahuayo. Wandering and a commercial instinct are important elements of Sahuayo's collective self-identity. According to a local joke, when Neil Armstrong stepped from the *Eagle* lunar landing module and was about to drive the North American flag into lunar soil and proclaim himself the first man on the moon, he heard a Sahuayan pass by with his herd crying, "Pigs for Sale! Pigs for Sale!"[22]

The New Transnational Media: "Sahuayo, California"

The long-term migrants who tend to be the most active leaders of Sahuayans in the United States did not live in Sahuayo during the period of political liberalization in the late 1980s and the 1990s. Living in California exposes migrants to alternative worldviews and political practices (Castañeda 1993), but it also may isolate migrants from political changes in their communities of origin. However, new technologies allow absent migrants to become better informed members of their communities of origin. "Real time" access to information is especially important to our understanding of extra-territorial citizenship, because it addresses one of the main

---

[22] I am grateful to Álvaro Ochoa Serrano for sharing this joke.

complaints of those who reject the principle of extra-territorial citizenship—namely, that absentees are ignorant of the daily public life of the community. While the transnational migration literature is replete with references to the effects of new technologies such as telephones and jet travel (R. Smith 1995, Sontag and Dugger 1998), the Internet is a new means of transnational communication. There are now three grassroots Internet Web sites created by Sahuayan migrants that truly create a transnational community where social and political information is exchanged in ways that compress space and time.

The captain of a Sahuayan soccer club in Orange County launched a bilingual Internet site in 1998 called "Sahuayo, California."[23] In two years of operation, it has received over 12,000 "hits" and messages from Sahuayans as far away as Argentina, Spain, and Japan. A directory of electronic mail addresses and telephone numbers lists sixty-five Sahuayans all over the United States and one in Sahuayo. There is a page with gossip and news from Sahuayo and its satellite communities, a chat room, general background information about Sahuayo, and a handful of advertisements for Sahuayan businesses in Orange County and Sahuayo.[24] The soccer captain works at a wrecking yard whose Anglo owner employs four Sahuayan workers and has hired other Sahuayans in the past. The owner pays the $20 monthly cost to operate the Web site. The site has a link to a commercial used-autoparts Web site operated by the owner, but the owner's reasons for designing and paying for the Sahuayo site appear to be more paternalistic than motivated by economic self-interest. He has encouraged the Sahuayan who provides the information used in the Web site to take computer classes, learn to manage the site himself, and find employment outside the wrecking business.

Several months after the site was established, the Sahuayan worker traveled to Sahuayo to solicit help from the local Internet service provider. After several months of inactivity, the site now

---

[23] www.gr8net.net/sahuayo/. Other Sahuayan sites are www.sahuayense.com and http://members.tripod.com/Sahuayo_Michoacan/.

[24] A similar Internet site and electronic mail bulletin board for the high-emigration town of Jerez, Zacatecas, generates a steady flow of information about the political, cultural, and social life of Jerezanos all over the United States and Zacatecas. The bulletin board allows Zacatecanos in the United States to coordinate visits to Jerez and to plan reunions of Jerezanos in the North. It is often used by Zacatecanos born in the United States who are interested in visiting or learning more about Jerez.

BIENVENIDOS A LA PAGINA DE

 SAHUAYO

Welcome to our Web site!

Sahuayo, California

This web site is for the people of Sahuayo, Mexico, that are now living in California.
Este sitio es para gente de Sahuayo, Mich. Que viven en California.

Parroquia del Sagrado Corazon

Tzacuatl-Ayotl
The artwork is by Leonardo Castaneda

Fiesta Patrias

We feature the people from Sahuayo at work and at play.
Presentamos a la gente de Sahuayo en el trabajo y la diversion.

Please use this Web site to keep in touch with friends and family.
Por favor use este sitio para comunicarse con su familia y amigos.

There is a directory for you to list your name and address so that
others from Sahuayo now living in California, can find you.
Favor de anotarse en nuestro directorio, para que otra gente de
Sahuayo que viven en California pueda encontrarlo.

Find the Restaurant's and Business's of People from Sahuayo.

Figure 3. Opening page of the "Sahuayo, California" Web site

has a stream of listings from Sahuayans, mostly but not exclusively in the United States. Sahuayans post listings of births, report soccer club scores from Sahuayan teams in Santa Ana, solicit information about traveling to Sahuayo, and even post personal ads seeking a mate. A message posted on the night of the July 2, 2000, elections crowed, "Sahuayo is with the PAN! Congratulations, Vicente Fox! Out with the PRI rats! Rats out! Out with the PRI!" Use of the Internet is growing steadily in Sahuayo, though it is still primarily used by the elite and university students. In July 1999, there were 150 regular subscribers with the local Internet service provider. An Internet café opened in July 1999 with ten computers and has attracted a steady stream of users. A similar Internet café has been open since 1998 in Jiquilpan, and a third opened in Sahuayo in 2000.

The transnational media also include newspapers. One of the three weekly newspapers in Sahuayo prominently lists a correspondent in Anaheim, Orange County. In six months as a correspondent, he has not sent a single article to the editor of the newspaper (his brother-in-law), though he did arrange a weekly advertisement for an Orange County charter bus company. The correspondent is one of the paper's financial supporters. The editor suggests that perhaps when the correspondent retires in three years, he will have more time to write. Clearly, the correspondent's position is a status symbol for the newspaper more than a reader service. Yet even symbolic correspondents build prestige for the editor in Sahuayo, underlining the interdependence of migrants and non-migrants. In December 1999, the editor met with Sahuayan migrant representatives living all over the United States to encourage them to write articles for the paper and find an economical way for Sahuayans in the United States to subscribe. He suggested sending a bundle of newspapers by an express courier service to migrant representatives in selected U.S. cities who would then distribute the paper.

The editor of a regional newspaper in Jiquilpan that also covers Sahuayo has met with members of the Inglewood Jiquilpense association to promote subscriptions to his newspaper. He cites the example of an entrepreneur in neighboring Venustiano Carranza who sends weekly issues of the local newspaper to the satellite community in Hawaiian Gardens near Los Angeles. Through these new media, migrants are able to diversify the kinds of information they receive about their communities of origin and remain engaged in local Mexican politics. They illustrate how new technologies such as the Internet, jet travel, the cheap international telephone call, and courier services allow migrants to maintain contacts with their communities of origin in ways that were impossible for migrants in previous eras.

A Transnational Collection Plate? Networks of Migrants and Priests

Considering the pervasive influence of the Catholic Church in Sahuayo, it is not surprising that the Church is also one of the most important institutional actors in the relationship between Sahuayo and its migrants. The Church's role is even more significant because it is one of the few transnational organizations that has the capacity to interact directly with migrants on both sides of the border. During the first waves of mass migration at the turn of the century, priests throughout Mexico feared that contact with the United States would contaminate migrants. Returning migrants were seen as potential agents of Protestantism, secularism, and moral decay. Many priests encouraged their congregations to stay in Mexico. As it became clear that mass migration would continue, Mexican priests forged closer relationships with migrants and began offering them special masses, often celebrated during a designated Day of the Absentees (Hernández Madrid 1999, Durand 1994).

The Church in the United States has encouraged migrants to maintain or develop ties with both sending and receiving areas. Lone migrants who are not rooted in a community are considered more likely to engage in behaviors, such as infidelity, that the Church proscribes. The Church hopes that by encouraging migrants to associate with other migrants from their hometowns, they will maintain their cultural and religious traditions and be less likely to fall prey to secularism and moral turpitude. One Sahuayan priest encourages Sahuayans in the United States to approach priests in Sahuayo if they feel that clergy in the United States are not responsive to their needs. Sahuayan priests can then address the problem in the North through official Church channels. At the same time as the Church encourages transnational ties, its efforts also integrate migrants into their receiving communities by making their lives more comfortable and building their social networks (Levitt 2000, author interviews 1999).

Two churches in Santa Ana are gathering points for Sahuayans, and many of the networks of collective migrant participation in Sahuayan public life are based on relationships between migrants and priests. Yet even these religious networks are multi-stranded and can reflect divisions. There is a long history of priests traveling to the United States to ask for financial contributions for churches in Sahuayo or to officiate rites such as first communions or baptisms. Sahuayans living in the United States frequently finance these visits. The visits are not only welcomed by Sahuayan migrants; they are expected. "If he is a good priest, he will come to visit the people," said one Sahuayan community leader in Los Angeles.

Yet clergy on both sides of the border are sensitive to the perception that some Mexican parish priests only visit migrants to pass a transnational collection plate. Several current priests and migrants angrily refer to former priests who went to Sahuayan satellite communities primarily to collect money rather than officiate rites or offer spiritual succor. A leading Sahuayan priest who actively promotes a stronger relationship between migrants and the Church in Sahuayo—without the fund-raising component—emphasizes, "It's not right that we go and exploit people who are already exploited." Some priests also feel that even if it is legitimate to raise funds among Sahuayan migrants, those funds should be spent on productive projects or charities rather than fiestas.

Leaders of the Church in Orange County are concerned that there are Mexican priests who officiate rites in the United States without requesting permission from U.S. parish priests. Performing marriages without sanction from the parish priest is illegal according to California law, while performing unauthorized rites such as baptisms violates Church rules. Church leaders see these practices as worse yet if there is an appearance of the transaction of rites for financial contributions. Officially, the Church leadership discourages any secondary fund-raising outside standard Church channels. Some U.S. parish priests ignore the fund-raising of Mexican priests if the latter do not perform rites. U.S. parish priests may also turn a blind eye if visiting Mexican priests officiate masses in private homes, as long as there is no quid-pro-quo fund-raising. Sahuayan priests generally do not contact their counterparts in U.S. parishes when they visit. Some of the Sahuayan clergy feel that North American priests have different communication styles and maintain such hurried schedules that interaction is uncomfortable. There is also a perception among some Sahuayan clergy that Spanish priests in the United States disrespect Mexicans. Most importantly, the transnational personal networks of Sahuayan priests obviate the need to work directly with U.S. parish priests.

One of the functions of migrant-priest networks is to encourage migrant participation in Sahuayan religious festivals such as the fiestas of the Virgin of Guadalupe and the patron saint, Santiago Apóstol. Veneration of the Virgin and Santiago are two of the essential markers of Sahuayan identity. Religious fiestas are important in many towns in Michoacán and elsewhere in Mexico, but they are especially central to the public life of Sahuayo (González 1979, author interviews 1999). Migrant participation in these two fiestas is one of the strongest ways to assert a moral extra-territorial citizenship rooted in a specific place. Migrant-funded church projects also demonstrate migrants' financial commitment to Sahuayo. The Church's encouragement of Sahuayan solidarity through migrants' expressions of Mexican religious and cultural traditions legitimates migrants' claims to extra-territorial citizenship. The stamp of the Church on these activities is the strongest possible mark of the participants' Mexican Catholic morality, which demonstrates that despite residence in the United States, migrants remain Mexicans and Sahuayans of good moral standing.

The Colonia Sahuayense

The most visible and long-lived transnational Sahuayan network is a loose formation called the Colonia Sahuayense, which sponsors one of the twelve days of the annual fiesta of the Virgin of Guadalupe in Sahuayo. Each day of the fiesta is sponsored by a different *gremio* (guild), such as the sandal makers or the merchants from the marketplace. Since the late 1950s, Sahuayans who live in the United States have sponsored the fiesta on December 5th. By the early 1960s, Sahuayan migrants had organized Colonias in Santa Ana, Merced, and Los Angeles to sponsor the fiesta. Several years later, Sahuayans in Chicago organized a Colonia. Accounts of the Colonia's formation vary. Some priests and current Colonia leaders claim that the Colonia Sahuayense was a migrant initiative, while others assert that the idea originated with a Sahuayan priest. All agree that individual priests with contacts in the North were crucial for the motivation and organization of the Colonia.

The Colonia raises funds in the United States throughout the year, usually by sponsoring dances and dinners where raffles and sales of food and drink are the main source of income. Colonia leaders contact other Sahuayans through telephone calls or at venues where Sahuayans concentrate, such as churches, Sahuayan-owned businesses, and soccer or baseball games where Sahuayan teams play. A diverse group of Sahuayans and their friends from other parts of Mexico attend Colonia events. Three hundred people attended a typical monthly fund-raiser held in 1999 at the home of a Sahuayan community leader in Pico Rivera, halfway between Santa Ana and Los Angeles. The host owns a pet shop in Los Angeles and a furniture factory in Sahuayo. After he first came to California in 1979, he rarely returned to Sahuayo, but now he flies there almost once a month on business. He explained that at the same time as the community raises money to help Sahuayo, fund-raising parties make life more enjoyable in the United States by bringing Sahuayans together. The fund-raisers allow Sahuayans to exchange information about business and job opportunities. Carlos González Gutiérrez, one of the architects of the consulate's Communities Abroad program, argues that the main function of many Mexican HTAs is to create a sense of community among migrants in the United States and that projects in Mexico are secondary (1995). These two functions reinforce each other in the case of Sahuayo.

The Colonia Sahuayense proclaims its identity in the December 5th fiesta through inclusive and exclusive identity displays. Identity displays are directed outward at an audience of non-migrants and other migrants, but they also strengthen a sense of belonging among the participants. Performances of belonging call forth the same reaction in the performers as they do in the audience (Austin 1975). On December 5, returning migrants parade through the streets as a group to assert their Sahuayan identity publicly. Family members sometimes march to represent absentees. Former migrants now settled in Sahuayo may also march in place of friends who cannot attend. During the procession, the participants display symbols of Mexico and Sahuayo, such as a Mexican flag emblazoned with the name of the "Colonia Sahuayense Residente en Indiana," banners of the Virgin of Guadalupe, and a banner showing the twin towers of the main cathedral in Sahuayo. Each Colonia has a separate banner that announces the specific satellite community of the residents parading behind it. Mariachis and school-aged dancers accompany the procession as fireworks explode in the background.

The Colonia serves as a representative of a corporate body of Sahuayans abroad. In 1999, the priest presiding over the parade explicitly recognized the marchers as representatives of all Sahuayans who live in the United States. He declared over the microphone to the crowd of thousands that lined the parade route, "I extend a welcome to the Colonia del Norte. These people have given up their work and time to come here. Not all in the North could come, but the Colonia represents them." Migrants in the North can vicariously experience the parade through videos that are filmed at the yearly fiestas of the Virgin and Patrón Santiago by a Cuban-American and sold to Sahuayans in greater Los Angeles.

The leaders of the Colonia tend to be middle-aged men who have lived in the United States for twenty years or more. The current 48-year-old president is a permanent U.S. resident who since 1973 has lived in the Los Angeles area, where he owns a home and works as a janitorial supervisor. He returns to Sahuayo at least once a year and owns another home there. As soon as his youngest child graduates from high school in three years, he intends to return to Sahuayo. One of the striking features of contemporary migrant associations studied in New York City and in California is that they are often formed by long-term settlers. The level of transnational practices is not necessarily a declining function of the length of U.S. residence. Settlement does not presuppose a rejection of the country of origin. For some, transnational practices are much more important than brief transitory phenomena as migrants settle in the United States. Conversely, transnational associational life may actually integrate migrants into their receiving communities by strengthening their social networks in the United States (Glick Schiller et al. 1992, Basch et al. 1994, Portes 1999).

Several of the leaders are blue-collar workers with well-paying jobs, but they can raise their class position dramatically by returning to Sahuayo as benefactors. Marginalization in the United States has been noted by other researchers as one of the most important reasons that migrants organize transnationally. Rouse argues that migrants from Aguililla, Michoacán, living in California maintain their transnational links as a means of circumventing their subordinate class and racial positions in the United States (1992). While the Sahuayan migrants in this study do not frame their participation in these terms, they often emphasize that they feel much freer in Sahuayo from the control of the U.S. government and that society's rigid social norms. The freedom to litter, drive after drinking, and have loud parties without being ticketed by the police is praised frequently and contrasted to a restricted life in the United States.

Motivations for transnational activities partly depend on diverse experiences in the North, but the identity displays themselves (such as the Virgin of Guadalupe procession) are claims to

Figure 4. Mariachis accompany the Colonia Sahuayense as it parades through the streets of Sahuayo on December 5, 1999 (*photo by David Fitzgerald*)

Figure 5. Leaders of the Colonia Sahuayense march on December 5, 1999, in the annual procession during the fiesta of the Virgin of Guadalupe (*photo by David Fitzgerald*)

Figure 6. The Colonia Sahuayense in Indiana parades through Sahuayo on December 5, 1999 (*photo by David Fitzgerald*)

Figure 7. A banner of the Colonia Sahuayense del Norte during the December 5, 1999, parade (*photo by David Fitzgerald*)

inclusion in that they assert a shared concern for Sahuayo that is not mitigated by physical absence. At the same time, inclusive identity displays may be purposefully or unintentionally exclusive. Returnees have set themselves apart from other Sahuayans by organizing themselves as the Colonia del Norte and spending thousands of dollars on the fiesta. Paradoxically, migrants are able to sidestep their marginalization in the United States by displaying in Mexico the wealth they could only earn in the North. A 30–year resident of California who skins chickens at a processing plant led one of the Colonias in the procession wearing a fashionable new suit and jewelry. Vacationing returnees buy rounds of drinks and throw street parties for their neighborhoods. Even when their savings are minimal, returning migrants assert material success to the point that some are bankrupt by the end of their vacation and must borrow money to return to the United States.

When one former migrant who owns a business in Sahuayo was asked if norteños in the United States invest in the Sahuayan economy, he snorted that "they invest in drinking" when they come for vacation. "They come in their nice cars, but people here say they are conch shells—pretty on the outside, ugly inside.... They were born in Mexico, but they don't like anything here. They are no longer Sahuayans. They are Michoacanos of convenience so they can buy land, but they don't have any love for their country.... In practice, they are from neither here nor there." Although he underlined the importance of family remittances to the Sahuayan economy, he prefers that migrants stay in the United States and only send money, because they drive up the prices of housing when they return.

Many other Sahuayans do not share his resentments, and they welcome returning migrants with open enthusiasm. Yet displays by migrants that set them apart from non-migrants create a common impression that long-term migrants have adopted what are widely perceived as the consumerist, ostentatious values of the United States. Thus identity displays are a double-edged sword. A parade that is ostensibly an inclusive identity display may have the unintended consequence of delegitimating the Sahuayanness of migrants in the eyes of some non-migrant Sahuayans.

Sahuayans tend to reserve their harshest criticisms for migrant youths. Norteño youths are widely blamed for a perceived wave of gang crime and drug use in Sahuayo over the last ten years. During one interview, a Sahuayan businessman and community leader lashed out at migrants and the influence of American culture more generally. He blamed drugs, new attitudes, new religions, and delinquency on U.S. influences transmitted by return migrants, television, and tourists. "There were practically no bad people in Sahuayo before!" he said. While his comments are hyperbolic, the perception of a Sahuayo corrupted by norteño youths is a common concern. Sahuayans point to graffiti from Santa Ana gangs such as the Lopers, which is scrawled on walls around town. As quoted by a local newspaper, the ranking priest in Sahuayo blamed returning emigrants for contaminating the fiesta of the Patrón Santiago by wearing grotesque masks and dressing as pregnant women. Inclusive identity displays such as the procession of the Colonia become even more important as migrants seek to counter the image that they have been corrupted by America and have lost their Sahuayan morality.

The Colonia has recently tried to project another image of norteño youths through the selection of a "Queen of the North." The use of young women to represent their (or their parents') communities of origin is a ubiquitous feature of HTAs in the United States, and it is usually discussed by HTA leaders and researchers in the context of encouraging the second generation of immigrants to identity with the community of origin (R. Smith 1995, Zabin and Escala Rabadán 1998). The use of hometown queens should also be examined as an attempt by migrants to demonstrate to their communities of origin that their children are not gangsters and that they continue to hold the moral values of their Mexican communities. It is not coincidental that women are used to symbolize moral purity and tradition, in contradistinction to the negative images of norteño youths that primarily revolve around young men. Women are often the bearers of notions of tradition and morals.

The Colonia Sahuayense in Los Angeles selected a Queen of the North in 1998 from among five candidates who sold tickets for the competition. The winner was born in Sahuayo but left to live in Los Angeles when she was one year old. She returned to Sahuayo after her selection to ride in an open car during the December 5th parade and to attend the Colonia-sponsored fiesta at the town jail. Although she had regularly visited Sahuayo for summer vacations, she said the act of returning as the Queen made her feel even more proud to be Sahuayan. She said she did not take offense when she was teased in Sahuayo as "The Queen of the Cholos." The $900 she raised selling tickets to support her candidacy was spent mostly on her airfare and special clothing. The 1999 contest was canceled part way through because the six candidates did not raise sufficient funds to pay for a queen's expenses. As the following chapter will explain, however, HTA pageants can be an important source of income for developing transnational projects.

When the Colonia raises excess funds, it donates them to a church in Sahuayo for renovation expenses or to a home for the elderly. The Colonia is currently raising $4,000 on its own initiative for a new front door to one of the churches. When a priest balked at putting a plaque on the door in recognition that it was a contribution of the Colonia, a Colonia leader threatened to withdraw the funding. Only after securing a promise of recognition did fund-raising continue. In the 1970s and 1980s, the Colonia also raised funds for a Catholic dispensary, the construction of classrooms at a Catholic school, and donations of food and blankets to poor Sahuayans. The Colonia no longer dispenses goods in public, however, in part because of an incident several years ago in which some Sahuayans waiting in line for donations scuffled with norteños when the supply was exhausted. The Chicago Colonia gave charity aid to some of Sahuayo's poorest neighborhoods several years ago (Espinosa 1999), but in 1999 it was not developing any new projects.

For the last seven years, the Colonia as a whole has sponsored musical groups that perform on December 5th in the courtyard of the town jail. In 1999, about fifty migrants joined over one hundred prisoners in an hour-long fiesta. While some prisoners danced to the music, others circulated among the migrants selling handmade crafts and soliciting cigarettes. The Colonia also sponsored a free lunch for the prisoners the day before. Migrant patronage of these activities is well publicized; Colonia leaders, followed by a brass band playing at high volume, lead a procession through the streets to the jail.

Collective migrant patronage of processions and projects goes beyond displaying shared community symbols. Migrant economic participation in the community through projects and remittances is another potential legitimization of extra-territorial citizenship claims. Among Sahuayan politicians who accept the principle of extending suffrage in Mexican presidential elections to Mexicans living abroad, migrant remittances are one of the most frequently cited reasons for this right of citizenship. Non-migrant Sahuayans who support local forms of extra-territorial citizenship for absent Sahuayans also cite the importance of remittances. Both family remittances and group remittances by an organization such as the Colonia are considered a sign of continued interest and involvement in the community.

Economic participation as citizenship legitimization has its limits, however. Many non-migrant Sahuayan elites take an instrumental view of extra-territorial citizenship. They are willing to accept absent migrant participation in Sahuayan public projects insofar as migrants provide funding, but they reject a fuller measure of extra-territorial citizenship, such as the extension of the vote abroad. For this large segment of elites, migrant economic participation is not the legitimization of full citizenship, but rather the *object* that explains their grudging acceptance of a truncated extra-territorial citizenship. Migrant economic participation also must appear altruistic if that participation is to legitimate migrant citizenship. Migrants must avoid the appearance that they are attempting to "buy" citizenship, because the perception of buying citizenship would violate the moral dimension of citizenship based on affective ties and a shared community identity.

The economic participation of the Colonia throughout the United States is weakening, however, for external and internal reasons. There were no development or philanthropic projects under consideration in 1999. The current president of the Colonia says that the needs of Sahuayo's poor are so great that the Colonia could never help all of them. Twenty years ago, the Colonia raised an average of $20,000 a year in Santa Ana and thousands more from the Colonias in other U.S. cities. In 1999, all of the Colonias together raised only $16,000. Most of this money is spent on mariachis, flowers, firecrackers, and other costs of the December 5th fiesta. Over the last ten years, fewer norteños have returned to Sahuayo to march in the parade. In 1999, less than fifty people marched, even though many more norteños returned to Sahuayo for the fiesta.[25] Norteños who have not contributed financially to the Colonia are often embarrassed to march, underlying the way that expenditure legitimates participation in the public expression of a Sahuayan identity. Migrant children born in the North tend to be less enthusiastic about the fiesta than are their parents, and new absenteeism policies in Santa Ana schools are a deterrent for parents to take their children out of class in early December. The Sahuayan priests traditionally most active in making trips to the United States to raise funds and motivate Sahuayans to continue participating in the fiesta have died or been reassigned to other posts.

---

[25] In all diasporas, a small core has an influence greater than its numbers for representing the diaspora to others and creating a sense of diaspora among potential diasporans (Tölölyan 1996).

Sahuayans in the United States who were once involved in the Colonia are now sometimes reluctant to give their time and money because of the widespread perception that former Colonia leaders in Santa Ana and Chicago-Indiana misappropriated funds for their personal use. Current leaders of the Colonia in Chicago warn that if norteño interest in the fiesta does not increase, 1999 will have been the last year that money was raised. The Colonia is almost moribund in Santa Ana, and many Sahuayans who live there are not sure if it still exists. The current president of the Colonia in Santa Ana was appointed by a priest in Sahuayo following the annual mass for migrants in May 1999. The appointment deviated from the normal procedures of the Colonia, in which each satellite community elects the board of directors of the Colonia by secret, democratic vote.[26] When the leadership structure of the Colonia falters, Sahuayan priests assert their influence to rebuild the organization.

Nevertheless, Sahuayan priests have not assumed control over the finances of the Colonia to create greater confidence among supporters. This is a departure from procedures elsewhere in the region, such as Francisco Sarabia, a village of 2,200 inhabitants three kilometers from Sahuayo. In Sarabia, a transnational network between migrants in Santa Ana and the Sarabia church relies on the priest to control funds raised for projects in Sarabia. The priest travels to Santa Ana to raise money for donations of food and blankets, church renovation, and a meeting hall that is owned by the church but used for all kinds of community functions. A lay coordinator in Santa Ana gathers Sarabians at public parks, private homes, and restaurants for masses or fiestas when the priest visits. The priest gives contributors receipts and then returns with the cash to Sarabia, where he reads aloud a list of donors at the end of mass.

The priest claims that Sarabian migrants are more likely to initiate or support projects with practical concerns for daily life rather than church renovations. In working to develop projects with municipal authorities and migrants, however, the priest is concerned that the municipal government will lower its public works budget in proportion to rising group remittances. The dan-

---

[26] In addition to the board of directors of each city's Colonia, there is a president of the Colonia for the entire United States. The current general president is the president of the Los Angeles Colonia, though in past years the general president has been the president of the Colonia in Santa Ana or Merced.

ger in projects financed by migrants from Sarabia and elsewhere is that group remittances will replace, rather than supplement, government spending. The unintended consequences of such projects would be to make governments less accountable to the demands of the citizenry by eliminating a measure of government responsibility for social welfare and development.

Although Francisco Sarabia is only three kilometers from Sahuayo and has a large satellite community in Santa Ana, the collective action networks of the two towns are separate. Sahuayans married to Sarabians living in Santa Ana may attend Sarabian events there, but there are no cooperative projects between the two towns or their migrants. The current Sarabian priest was formerly based in Sahuayo. During his 17–year stint, he raised practically all of the funds to build a new church from Sahuayans in the United States, mostly in Santa Ana. Since leaving Sahuayo, he has not contacted Sahuayans in Santa Ana, even when he goes to Santa Ana to visit Sarabians.

Sahuayan transnational religious networks also are fractured. In the 1980s, a 64-year-old blue-collar Sahuayan worker who has lived in Santa Ana since 1972 organized fund-raising for the July fiesta of the patron saint. He already was active in the Colonia Sahuayense and used the same personal networks to solicit funds directly for an informal group called Devotees of the Patrón Santiago Living in Santa Ana. Leaders of the Colonia saw his efforts as competing with their own project, and the two networks did not cooperate. For sixteen years, the Devotees raised funds for the Patrón Santiago fiesta and dispensed free meals to the poor, but the founder abandoned the effort because he felt there was a lack of interest among migrants and because the work was too time-consuming. He also suspected that funds he raised for a new church devoted to the Patrón Santiago were not used for their stated purpose, and he differed with a Sahuayan priest over the organization of the fiesta. Although he is a naturalized U.S. citizen, he holds dual Mexican nationality and returns to Sahuayo every July for the patron saint festival. He once thought that he would eventually return to Sahuayo but has now decided to stay in Santa Ana, where he no longer has much contact with other Sahuayans.

Many individual Sahuayan migrants continue to return for the fiesta of the Patrón Santiago and participate in the elaborate parades, but there is no longer any collective migrant presence.[27]

---

[27] Another organization of Sahuayans in Santa Ana is moribund as well. For six years during the 1980s, the Club Sahuayense sponsored an annual

More migrants return for the Patrón Santiago fiesta now than for the fiesta of the Virgin of Guadalupe, because the Santiago fiesta has a more carnival-esque atmosphere, and it is easier for migrants with established jobs or families in the North to take vacations in the summer. Domestic migrants have decreased their support for the fiesta of the Virgin as well. The Colonia Sahuayense in Guadalajara and Ocatlán, Jalisco, continues to organize a parade on December 12th, but the Colonia Sahuayense in Mexico City has not participated since the leaders of the gremio died. A former director of the government cultural center in Sahuayo derogatorily refers to Sahuayans in Mexico City as *"pinches chilangos"* who no longer care about Sahuayo. The negotiation of extra-territorial citizenship on the local level extends to domestic Mexican migrants.

A new generation of Sahuayan priests is trying to reestablish links with Sahuayan migrants in the United States. One priest recently took two month-long tours of Sahuayan communities in the North.[28] At least two North American parish priests in Orange County have visited Sahuayo. Mexican Catholics are being recruited to serve in Orange County, where there is a need for priests who speak fluent Spanish and understand religious customs in Mexico. In June 1999, 32-year-old Ramón Cisneros became the first Michoacano ordained in the county. Like 90 percent of his high school class in Sahuayo, he had migrated north. He crossed the border illegally and headed to Orange County, where he worked as a cook. Eleven years later, he had become a priest and U.S. citizen (Godines 1999). Scores of Sahuayans attended his ordination and a reception where mariachis sang Sahuayan songs and the hall filled with cries of *"Arriba Sahuayo!"*[29] A replica of the Patrón Santiago figured prominently in the procession through the church. After the transnational priest officiated his first mass in Santa Ana at another church with a large congregation of Sahuayans, he returned to Sahuayo as a triumphant native son. He led a procession of two hundred people from his parents' home to the cathedral, where he gave mass to a crowd of 1,500. Migrants and

---

marathon in Sahuayo. It gave out prizes and t-shirts and attracted runners from all over the republic. When the California economy declined in the late 1980s, the Club was disbanded.

[28] Earlier in his clerical career, the priest went north (without legal papers or permission from Church authorities) for a month-long vacation in which he saved up money for a car by washing dishes at a Los Angeles restaurant during the week and officiating mass at a local church on the weekends.

[29] "Up with Sahuayo!"

priests are still negotiating their economic and pastoral relationship, but there appears to be a consensus among parish priests and higher Church authorities in both Orange County and Michoacán that the clergy must learn to be as mobile and transnational as its congregations.

Migrants and Partisan Politics

While Sahuayan migrants are becoming less active in expressing their identification with Sahuayo publicly and collectively through religious festivals, political leaders in Sahuayo are attempting to forge better relations with Sahuayan migrants. Many political leaders are former migrants themselves. Most politicians with migration experience worked in the North as wage laborers when they were young men and then returned to open businesses in Sahuayo. A former panista municipal president worked in the construction industry in Los Angeles and Orange County throughout 1977; he earned enough to pay off his wedding debts and save $4,000 for a house and land in Sahuayo. He later returned to California frequently for training as an optician and to import equipment for his practice in Sahuayo. Another former panista municipal president worked in a Los Angeles garden furniture factory for two months in 1967, but he returned to Sahuayo where he eventually became a leading entrepreneur. Considering the high rates of migration among men in Sahuayo, it is not surprising that many politicians have worked in the United States. There is no indication that former migrants are more likely than non-migrants to become politicians.

When political leaders were queried about the effects of their migratory experience on their worldviews or political beliefs, their responses varied widely. Both former panista municipal presidents said their experiences made them appreciate the advantages of good organization, but it did not change their political views. Several other opposition political leaders said that their experience in the United States was a catalyst to work for changes in Mexico that would obviate the need for Mexicans to migrate. One young PAN activist who worked in a Los Angeles optics lab in 1998 said he was bothered by the sight of day workers standing on Los Angeles street corners waiting to be hired. "It's someone's fault they are there," he said. A former PAN municipal committee president described the humiliation of life as an undocumented restaurant worker in Los Angeles in the late 1970s, when he was forced to sleep in the restaurant and once spent five days in a Chula Vista jail awaiting deportation to Mexico. Now he owns a clothing store and vacations in the United States twice a year. Despite the hardships, he says his migratory experience did not change his political views. Migration experiences may have impacts that are not revealed by self-reporting, but none of the leaders spoke of a dramatic change in political attitudes such as those found by other researchers elsewhere in Mexican high-emigration sites.

In conducting oral histories among ejidatarios in Los Altos de Jalisco, Craig found that "the single most distinctive characteristic shared by the majority of the first agraristas is that they had worked in the United States before becoming ejidatarios, usually even before joining the agrarian reform" (Craig 1983: 178). The same personality traits that would motivate one to accept the risks and challenges of migration may have facilitated participation in the agrarian reform movement. Yet Craig found that the agraristas themselves saw their migratory experience as being seminal in the development of their political consciousness. The U.S. experience of higher wage scales, better living conditions, and better relationships between laborers and supervisors raised the expectations of migrants who returned to rural Jalisco. The literacy skills they developed in the United States also allowed them to sign petitions, write letters to government officials and agencies, and read about agrarian reform issues in newspapers and political tracts. While most of the migrants had not participated in strictly political activities in the United States, their changed and enlarged worldviews facilitated their participation in the agrarian reform movement (Craig 1983: 178–82). A similar tendency for the first agraristas to have been former migrants was found in diverse sending communities of Michoacán (Fonseca 1988: 363, Alarcón 1986: 182–84, Gledhill 1993).

Anecdotal evidence from a large cross-section of sending communities reveals that successful return migrants have used the wealth generated by their trips to the United States to gain social prestige and to contend for local political offices such as the municipal presidency, chief of police, and party posts (Alarcón 1988: 348, López Castro 1986: 111–12, Gledhill 1995: 205). At the same time, return migration has been blamed for increasing the social stratification of communities of origin by concentrating economic and political power in the hands of those who have access to dollars (Cornelius 1998a, Hernández Madrid 1988, Wiest 1979).

Municipal presidents from Sahuayo and the three surrounding municipios of Jiquilpan, Cojumatlán, and Venustiano Carranza have gone to the United States in their official capacities to visit satellite communities. These politicians tend to be sensitive to the suggestion that their visits are motivated by fund-raising, but they have lists of projects that they hope to develop with migrant aid. They especially seek migrant investment in the sending community economies. The Mexican consulates, through the Program for Mexican Communities Abroad, generally help to organize such visits. A panista municipal president from Sahuayo visited Chicago and Santa Ana in 1997 with the help of the consulates and his own personal network of friends and relatives. In a series of receptions and private parties organized by the consulates and old friends, the municipal president showed a video of the sandal industry in Sahuayo to encourage migrant investment. No concrete projects resulted from the visit, but the former president claims that the trip encouraged the Sahuayan community in Santa Ana to unite.

In July 1999, a visiting delegation from the Colonia Sahuayense in Chicago invited the new priísta municipal president of Sahuayo to visit Chicago. The president in turn invited all of the visiting Colonia leaders to a reception during the 1999 Virgin of Guadalupe fiesta, at which he urged them to cooperate with the municipio when planning their public activities. The Virgin of Guadalupe fiesta has both a civil and a religious aspect. While the municipio tried to organize the fiesta around the plaza as part of the plaza revitalization—one of the municipal president's most visible projects—church leaders have tried to maintain control by holding the fiesta at the Church of the Virgin of Guadalupe. The Colonia thus became involved in local Sahuayan political disputes despite its putatively apolitical nature.

The reception was an occasion for the municipal president to develop ties with Colonia leaders. He claims to be scheduling a visit to Santa Ana in 2000, organized through his personal network, and he sought the help of Colonia leaders to gather Sahuayans if he makes the trip. The municipal president says he wants to encourage Sahuayans in the United States to organize themselves and maintain their links with Sahuayo. Existing associations of Sahuayan migrants would be the basis for developing municipal projects such as creating a park or buying a good ambulance. Like leaders of all political parties in Sahuayo, one of the municipal president's goals is to encourage migrant investment. He says he also wants to inform Sahuayans about the consular services of the Mexican government so they feel represented and "don't feel unprotected." In more abstract terms, he is acknowledging that Sahuayans abroad deserve the protection of the community of Mexicans.

Despite the nascent relationship between Sahuayo's municipal president and Colonia leaders, Sahuayan migrants typically play a small role in Sahuayan party politics. One important exception was the campaign of the last failed PRD candidate for municipal president. During the campaign, this individual proposed that Sahuayans living in the United States elect a *regidor*[30] to represent migrant interests in the municipal government. The candidate also invited two California union leaders born in Mexico to participate in his electoral campaign in Sahuayo as advisers, in an effort to demonstrate the candidate's support for the working conditions of Sahuayans in the North. Local PRD leaders, reflecting the political position of their national party, seek to involve migrants—who already have "voted with their feet" by leaving Mexico—in Mexican politics as presumed supporters of the opposition. Historically, the PRD has been a weak party in Sahuayo; it is unlikely, therefore, that it will be able to enact its proposals in the near future.

PAN and PRI leaders in Sahuayo are divided equally in their support for political rights for Mexicans living in the United States. Among Sahuayan political leaders who accept more migrant participation, the primary legitimization of the migrants' thickened political membership is their economic power and their continued interest in Sahuayo as expressed through remittances. One prominent priísta, discussing how to attract migrant investment, proposed erecting a statue in the plaza to honor absent Sahuayans (author interview). "Physically they are there, but mentally they are here," he said. A statue would make them feel "taken into account" when they return. "Taking into account" suggests accepting an individual's right to an effective presence in the public sphere, to use Balibar's language (1988).

The inclusive discourse of many PAN and PRI leaders in encouraging migrant investment and aid to Sahuayan philanthropic and infrastructure projects changes dramatically, however, when they speak of the extension of suffrage to Mexicans abroad. Beyond ostensibly technical objections, the most common reason for rejecting the extension of suffrage in presidential elections is that Mexicans in the United States "don't live the same reality" as Mexicans in Mexico, and therefore do not understand Mexico's problems. According to this argument, the presumed ignorance of

---

[30] A *regidor* is roughly equivalent to a city council member.

Mexicans in the United States would make them susceptible to manipulation by Mexican political parties, the U.S. media, or the U.S. government. The same priísta who wants Sahuayans abroad to feel "taken into account" claims that in regards to the vote, "one must be limited by the fact of being abroad."

There is a class dimension to objections against the full participation of migrants abroad that is usually unstated. The wage differential between the United States and Mexico potentially allows dramatic class mobility for returning migrants, who are suddenly on an economic par with non-migrant elites. A 31-year-old lawyer who is the president of the PRI's municipal committee explained his objection to the right to vote abroad in the following terms:

> It's not that I don't want to give them [Sahuayans in the United States] space, but there are different lifestyles. A gardener in the United States might live better than I do. They don't live the same reality. If I live here, I know what's going on. I can't give my opinion about another house. Those who live in the house make the decisions in the house. Other people visit. This is how it should be on the national level.

All of the Sahuayan political leaders interviewed accept the participation of Sahuayans who return permanently, but many do not want interference from Sahuayans who live primarily in the United States. As one panista leader explained succinctly, "If they want to participate, let them come here." The Michoacano federation in Chicago has faced similar opposition to some of its projects from non-migrants. Víctor Espinosa stated the problem in his report of the Chicago-Michoacán Project. "In some communities, there are minority groups that oppose the idea that migrants, because they spend more time in Chicago, return to resolve the problems that supposedly only concern people who stay in the community" (Espinosa 1999, my translation).

Leaders of the PRI and PAN almost universally reject the notion of Sahuayans abroad voting in municipal elections, citing both technical and conceptual objections. Some elites who would accept the vote abroad in federal elections reject the vote abroad in municipal elections because, they say, absent migrants are not sufficiently familiar with local politics or politicians. While there are sources of information in the United States about Mexican presidential politics, they allege that the same level of information does not exist in regard to local politics. PRD leaders suggest that the technical barriers might be insurmountable, but in theory they support the extension of suffrage abroad to include municipal elections. They even mention the possibility of one day using the Internet to allow Sahuayans in the North to vote in municipal elections. New technologies such as the "Sahuayo, California" Internet page, transnational subscriptions to local newspapers, telephones, and videos allow absent migrants to be much more aware of their towns' public life. Technology has the potential not only to increase the frequency of contacts between sending and receiving communities, but also to allow qualitative changes in transnational practices such as citizenship.

Dual nationality further delegitimizes any political rights in Mexico in the eyes of some Sahuayan political elites who are otherwise willing to accept the vote abroad. This group says that nationality is an identity. "You are either Mexican or North American," said one priísta official. "One cannot be both." It appears that most political leaders are less interested in encouraging a citizenship that transcends borders than in seeking alternative sources of income for local government and prophylactic protection for their parties in case suffrage is extended abroad.

The arguments of Sahuayan elites who reject the full citizenship of absent Sahuayans often appeal to a Greek model of citizenship in which citizenship is participatory, based on duty as well as rights, and territorially bound (Pocock 1998, Oldfield 1998). Many political elites assert that Sahuayans abroad do not have the right to a public voice in Sahuayo because they do not know what is happening in Sahuayo. For these elites, citizenship is based on daily participation in the public life of the polis. Others say that political participation cannot be a right without commensurate public duties. Because migrants are physically outside the polity, it is impossible to coerce them into fulfilling their duties. Absent migrants cannot be citizens in the Greek sense by virtue of their absence.

The question of the rights and obligations of citizenship is an old one, but it takes on special significance in the transnational sphere. Legal obligations can ultimately only be enforced by coercion, and international boundaries severely limit a state's ability to coerce its citizens. Without legal obligations, it is much harder to argue for legal rights. As one panista politician and entrepreneur said of Sahuayans abroad, "They don't have any obligation, so they don't have any rights." Many Sahuayan migrants, and some non-migrants, claim that Sahuayans have a moral obligation to their community. A 22–year resident of Santa Ana who has participated in past charity collections for Sahuayo and returns every July asserted that "the people in our town have the right to the same services as us." Moral obligations imply that rights will be moral as well. Moral does not merely mean symbolic, however. The examples of migrant patronage of projects and the stakes involved in terms of property rights and community recognition demonstrate that the moral has concrete manifestations.

Sahuayans living in Santa Ana generally favor the rights to dual nationality and the vote abroad, but none of the Sahuayans interviewed was actively demanding a greater voice in Sahuayan partisan political life. Except insofar as the visits by municipal presidents are unstated promotions of their parties, transnational political relations are not partisan. Leaders of the Colonia Sahuayense in Santa Ana, Los Angeles, and Chicago stress that the Colonia is apolitical, and for a former Santa Ana Colonia representative in Sahuayo it is "anti-political." Many leaders of the Colonia and other transnational civil networks that raise funds in Santa Ana are visibly uncomfortable when queried about partisan politics.

Now more than ever, the Colonia Sahuayense in Santa Ana and Los Angeles is a group strictly dedicated to the fiesta of the Virgin. Migrant Sahuayans could potentially convert their participation into political capital by using their symbolic capital,[31] economic power, and assertion of continued identification with Sahuayo as a legitimizing mechanism for deeper influence in Sahuayo. However, the Colonia is barely able to raise money for buying firecrackers and flowers, much less to form the base of a transnational social movement. The perception among Sahuayan migrant leaders that politics is dirty and corrupt contributes to a narrow vision of the Colonia's role in Sahuayo. The rejection of anything migrants consider "political" is prominent in many other networks or HTAs whose members insist on the strictly "cultural" nature of their project, even when those activities are patently political.[32] The kinds of extra-territorial citizenship claims in Sahuayo are likely to be negotiations over moral rights of property protections and ac-

---

[31] "Symbolic capital" represents the "acquisition of a reputation for competence and an image of respectability and honourability that are easily converted into political positions as a local or national notable" (Bourdieu 1986: 291).

[32] The Federation of Zacatecan Clubs almost split in 1998 over a debate within its membership regarding the degree to which its activities should be "political" (Zabin and Escala Rabadán 1998).

ceptances of a common identity, rather than forms of legal citizenship or overt partisan political participation.

The rejection of "politics" in the narrow sense is one factor among many that has prevented a relationship between the Colonia Sahuayense and the Mexican consulate. The Chicago Colonia registered with the consulate in 1997 when the federation of Michoacano HTAs was formed, but the Colonias in Los Angeles and Santa Ana have never registered. Some Sahuayans in Santa Ana and Los Angeles see the consulate as a political organ that at best will stifle organizational activities with bureaucratic interference and at worst might damage the interests of migrants who register. A few Sahuayans privately say they fear that one day the consulate itself could cooperate with the U.S. Immigration and Naturalization Service (INS) to deport undocumented Mexicans.[33] Zabin and Escala Rabadán suggest that Michoacán's history as a cauldron of PRD dissent may be a reason for the low level of contact between Michoacanos and the consulate in Los Angeles (1998).

Transnational Civil Society: The Continuing Role of the State

The ability of Sahuayans living in the United States to develop projects in Sahuayo is hampered by their lack of cooperation with the Mexican government, as the following examples illustrate. Even in an era of transnational migration and economic globalization, the state remains an important actor.

In 1997, the 50-year-old president of Cruz Ambar, a voluntary paramedic corps in Sahuayo, raised $5,000 among a network of his Sahuayan friends in Santa Ana to buy an ambulance. Although he had a wide base of personal contacts built in countless trips between Santa Ana and Sahuayo since 1971, it was difficult to obtain institutional support. He approached a priest in Santa Ana to raise funds at a church, but he was rebuffed on the grounds that the Church generally tries to avoid secondary collections for non-Church projects. The president finally raised the funds from about one hundred contributors, eighty of whom were Sahuayans and

---

[33] Such fears have some basis in historical precedent. During the 1930s, the consulate cooperated with U.S. immigration authorities to repatriate hundreds of thousands of Mexicans. This cooperation later limited the consulate's capacity to lead *mutualista* organizations (Rivera Salgado 1999).

the remainder, immigrants from other parts of Mexico. After raising the money, he discovered that to avoid hefty import taxes, he needed a registered organization or government agency in the United States to sponsor the importation of the ambulance into Mexico. Because there is no registered association of Sahuayans in Santa Ana, he solicited the help of the city of Santa Ana and the Mexican consulate—without success. He then turned to the Federation of Jalisciense Clubs, which was willing to sponsor the ambulance if he registered Cruz Ambar with the federation. "It's shameful that I had to ask the Jaliscienses for help because the Sahuayans here are so disorganized," he later said.

The Cruz Ambar president was finally able to buy an ambulance in León, Guanajuato, and avoid the importation problem. The ambulance is the only functioning unit in the Sahuayo area that serves the public regardless of whether they have health insurance. On the December 5th following the purchase, the ambulance was driven in the Colonia procession with a sign taped to the rear window thanking the "colony and family of Sahuayans living in the United States" for their aid. One of the largest donors to the ambulance fund is a middle-aged businessman who first worked as a gardener and janitor in Dallas when he was twenty years old but now owns a produce store, candy store, and bridal shop in Santa Ana. He returns to Sahuayo several times a year for business and vacation. Although he has contributed to several philanthropic projects in Sahuayo and the region, he is an intensely private man who insists on anonymity. Nevertheless, the public recognition of the ambulance as donated by "the norteños" as a corporate group creates symbolic capital for all Sahuayans abroad, even if the individual donor is not recognized.

In May 1999, the Cruz Ambar president returned to Santa Ana to raise money for another ambulance and a school bus for handicapped children. He carried photos of the first ambulance driving in the December 5th parade as proof that funds were used for their stated purpose, but he still faced the problem of importing any vehicle he bought in the United States. The Zacatecan owner of the auto shop where he works intermittently has agreed to form a registered association in Santa Ana of the Sahuayo Cruz Ambar delegation. Although he is Zacatecan, the shop owner says he wants to help Mexico any way he can, given that the Mexican government "only robs its people" through high taxes. Like one of the major Sahuayan donors, the Zacatecan says Mexicans must rely on themselves to improve their communities. They cannot rely on the government. The Cruz Ambar president has publicly charged the

Figure 8. An ambulance purchased by Cruz Ambar with $5,000 donated by migrants in Santa Ana drives through the streets of Sahuayo in 1997 during the annual Colonia Sahuayense procession (*photo by Cruz Ambar*)

Figure 9. Poster on the rear of the ambulance reads: "Our thanks to the colony and family of Sahuayans living in the United States of America for their help in obtaining this vehicle" (*photo by Cruz Ambar*)

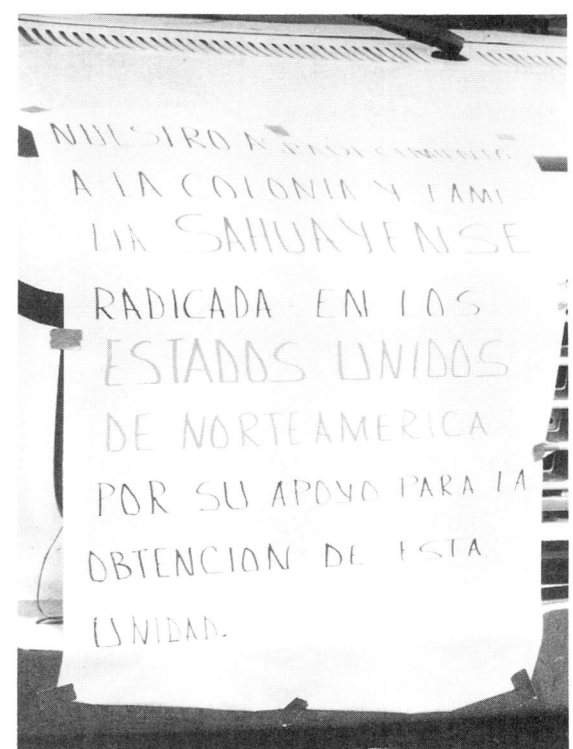

Mexican government with human rights abuses and a lack of attention to its citizens. Nevertheless, Cruz Ambar is forced to work with the government to execute transnational projects successfully. The Cruz Ambar president carries a letter from the municipal president of Sahuayo asking Mexican customs to cooperate in the importation of any Cruz Ambar vehicle, but it seems that a more institutionalized relationship would be more effective.

Actors in a separate transnational network, which had no cooperative relationship with the state, failed in a similar transnational undertaking, and in the process they indirectly strained the confidence of Sahuayan migrants in California. Ten years ago, a delegation from a private Catholic hospital in Sahuayo flew to Los Angeles and Santa Ana to raise money to buy second-hand medical equipment. A Sahuayan in Los Angeles arranged for the delegation to purchase equipment at reduced prices from a Los Angeles County clinic that was closing. To avoid paying Mexican import taxes on the equipment, the delegation sent a trailer-truck full of equipment to the border at Nuevo Laredo, Tamaulipas. Nuevo Laredo was chosen as the port of entry, despite forcing a detour of hundreds of kilometers from the most direct route, because the delegation had Sahuayan contacts in Mexican customs there who could allow the equipment to pass without paying taxes. One hundred kilometers from Nuevo Laredo, the truck overturned and destroyed almost all of the equipment.

When part of the damaged equipment eventually arrived at the hospital in Sahuayo, some of the doctors did not believe the story of the overturned truck. They suspected that members of the delegation or other doctors had sold the working equipment for profit and then delivered the damaged equipment to avert suspicion. Those claims could not be substantiated, but broken x-ray machines, incubators, anesthesia units, and other pieces of useless equipment are still scattered around the hospital. After the incident, Sahuayans in Santa Ana and Los Angeles lost interest in raising funds and donating their time to hospital projects.

The experiences of Cruz Ambar and the hospital delegation suggest that transnational projects that involve the physical movement of goods across national borders are very difficult to carry out without at least minimal cooperation from the state. Even when HTAs cooperate with the Mexican consulate, obtaining the paperwork from Mexican customs to transport goods for public projects can take months. Transnational networks have not superseded the state, which remains one of many institutions that regulate or influence transnational activities (Levitt 1999).

Another mechanism pursued by Sahuayans is the establishment of sister-city relationships. In the late 1970s, a group of Sahuayans living in Lancaster, California, visited the mayor of Sahuayo to propose that Lancaster and Sahuayo become sister cities. The governments of both cities agreed to the plan and exchanged delegations. In two visits to Lancaster, the Sahuayan delegation found few Sahuayans but was welcomed by Jaliscienses from Ocatlán and Poncitlán, which are near Sahuayo. Over the next five years, Lancaster donated a 1951 Ford fire engine (described by current Sahuayo volunteer firefighters as "a pretty relic"), fire-fighting equipment rumored to have been diverted by a former Sahuayan municipal president, and a street sweeper. Because Sahuayans park their cars along the curb, where trash tends to collect, the street sweeper drove up and down the middle of the main boulevard, serving no useful function until it was given to Mexico City following the 1985 earthquake. City officials in Lancaster and Sahuayo no longer contact each other. With projects that do not take into account the needs of Sahuayo and without mechanisms of accountability, the sister-city relationship has not been very productive.

Sahuayan Migrants and the 2000 Elections

The participation of migrants in Mexican partisan politics became a renewed subject of interest during the 2000 election campaign. As described in chapter 3, even if all of the ballots cast at special polling sites along the northern border were cast by migrants (which they definitely were not), the ballots at these special sites would only represent a minute fraction of the total presidential vote. How did migrants influence the vote in the Mexican interior, directly or indirectly? Anecdotal evidence gathered in Sahuayo near election day suggests that virtually no migrants who generally live in the United States returned to Sahuayo to vote. Neither did I find evidence of strong partisan appeals by telephone, e-mail, or letters. Still, at least some shuttle migrants participated in the election as voters and even as party activists.

The major return flow of migrants for the summer—for the fiesta of the Patrón Santiago—occurred several weeks after the elections. Even for those U.S.–based migrants who were in Sahuayo on election day, there were several barriers to participation. Many Sahuayan migrants are unable to vote. A few are no longer Mexican citizens, having adopted U.S. citizenship. Mexicans historically have had one of the lowest naturalization rates of any immigrant group in the United States (González Baker et al. 1998), though there has been a wave of defensive naturalizations in response to changes in U.S. immigration law and a generally hostile political environment. In 1995, following the passage in California of Proposition 187, citizenship applications in Los Angeles rose by a factor of five (Uhlaner 1996). U.S. federal legislation in 1996 increased the disadvantages of U.S. residence without citizenship by restricting non-citizen access to social services and making non-citizens subject to deportation for an expanded range of crimes. Anecdotal evidence suggests that Sahuayans have followed the tendency of Mexican immigrants to naturalize in increasing numbers.

However, there are legal and psychological barriers to naturalization. The process of naturalization can take several years, even after the five-year residency requirement has been met. Many Sahuayans say they plan to return to Mexico after working in the United States, and they do not want to lose their Mexican citizenship. There also appears to be a high level of misinformation about U.S. and Mexican law. For instance, one young woman who lived briefly in Santa Ana before returning to Sahuayo said she would never become a U.S. citizen because she refuses to trample the Mexican flag. She swore that a friend of hers had seen Mexicans forced to trample their flag as one of the requirements when they took the oath of U.S. citizenship. Complicated immigration laws can also change rapidly. A 27–year resident of Los Angeles who owns homes in Los Angeles and Sahuayo said he was afraid to take U.S. citizenship because he did not want to lose his property rights in Sahuayo. Although the 1996 constitutional reform allowing dual nationality for Mexicans allows dual nationals full property rights, such information is not widely known. A solution pursued by some migrants is to achieve a de facto form of extrajudicial dual citizenship. Two informants said their family members register their U.S.–born children in Sahuayo as if they were born in Mexico. While it is impossible to know how common this practice is, such a strategy would allow the children to assume the advantages of citizenship in both countries when they become adults.[34]

---

[34] In another case of autonomous de facto "dual citizenship," an elected official in Michoacán said he had voted in a U.S. election after completing all of the U.S. naturalization requirements but before taking the oath of citizen-

Of those who have Mexican citizenship, many do not have the required IFE voting credential. According to a local IFE official, there is a spike in voting credential applications in December and January, when many migrants return to Michoacán. Because it takes four to six weeks to process a credential, many migrants return to the North before their credentials are ready. If the applicant does not pick up his or her credential in person within two years, the IFE destroys the document and the applicant must start the process over from the beginning. Many migrants never return for their credential. According to the official, the object for many migrants is not the voting credential itself. They only want a temporary receipt of application that can be used to obtain a passport, even though the temporary document does not allow voting.

A migrant who intends to vote must plan far in advance. For example, one Sahuayan who lives in Los Angeles applied for the voting credential while he was in Sahuayo in July for a family funeral. His plan was to return to Sahuayo in December for the Virgin of Guadalupe fiesta and pick up the credential at that time. Barring any changes in the law, he will have to return to Sahuayo thereafter to cast his ballot in an election. Anecdotal evidence from multiple sources suggests that many Sahuayan migrants in the North who already have the IFE credential are illegal immigrants. These individuals are afraid to return to Mexico to vote because it would be dangerous and costly for them to reenter the United States illegally. Considering these many obstacles, it is not surprising that so few Sahuayans living in the United States have sought to vote in Mexican elections.

It is more difficult to gauge the influence that U.S.–based migrants have on the votes of their family members and friends in Sahuayo. Anecdotal evidence shows that some Sahuayans did discuss the elections with migrants in the United States. Most migrants appeared to support Vicente Fox, whom they hoped would improve the Mexican economy, fight corruption, and open the political system by bringing a different political party to power for the first time in seventy-one years. One Sahuayan sending greetings from *"Gringolandia"* on the "Sahuayo, California" Web site congratulated Mexico and the PAN on "the triumph of democracy." Some former migrants and non-migrants insisted that migrants in the North had tremendous influence. "Norteños have a lot of influence here. They have lived in a democratic country, and

---

ship. He said he was misled by the organization offering citizenship classes and would never have voted had he known he was still ineligible.

they begin to know their rights. They see how poorly Mexicans live," said a municipal government employee whose three brothers are in California, a place where he himself has vacationed but never worked.

Even those who felt migrants were influential, however, could not point to specific cases of Sahuayan migrants calling to influence the vote in the manner that both Fox and Cárdenas sought during their campaign trips in the United States. Several Sahuayan migrants contacted in California said they had discussed the elections with their family members, but they did not make adamant partisan appeals. Other Sahuayans, including returned migrants, said their family members and friends in the North did not show any interest in the elections. "They no longer care about what happens here," said a taxi driver who had recently returned from Santa Ana. There was no discernible pattern that would explain the polarized perceptions of indirect migrant influence on the elections. More extensive in-depth interviews in both Sahuayo and destination sites in the United States would be necessary to measure the indirect influences of U.S.–based migrants on voting behaviors, but it appears that strong partisan appeals were not common.

Some shuttle migrants were very active in the elections, however. The Cruz Ambar official who brought the ambulance to Sahuayo was a coordinator for PRD representatives at ten polling sites. He said that his thirty-one years as a part-time migrant in Santa Ana have exposed him to different ideas about the world, but he would not offer specifics. Another shuttle migrant, 46-year-old Leonardo, has made dozens of trips to Orange County, Las Vegas, and even Hawaii over the last twenty-four years. He is a legal permanent resident of the United States, where he works as a hotel employee or gardener, but he maintains a house, family, and clothing store in Sahuayo. Leonardo said he voted for the PRD congressional candidates according to his personal convictions, but he strategically cast his presidential ballot for Fox in order to support the opposition candidate most likely to win. He had discussed the elections with migrants in California on a trip north a month earlier, and he said they had the same concerns he did. "We are here [California] because the Mexican government steals everything," he said. Mexican citizens like Leonardo and the Cruz Ambar activist lead truly transnational lives and can fully participate in Mexican politics.

In the 1994 presidential election, the PAN narrowly led the PRI by 47 to 45 percent in Sahuayo, with the PRD taking 6 percent (IFE

2000b). The PAN and its coalition partner trounced the PRI by a two-to-one margin in the 2000 presidential election, winning approximately 61 percent versus the PRI's 32 percent and the PRD's 6 percent of the Sahuayo vote.[35] Surprisingly, the PAN candidate for federal deputy also won a seat in the 2000 election, despite the district's inclusion of PRI and PRD strongholds like Jiquilpan. The deputy-elect, 47-year-old Francisco Ortiz of Los Reyes, and his 26-year-old *suplente*,[36] Ricardo Sánchez Gálvez of Sahuayo, will replace the current priísta deputy.

During the closing PAN campaign rally in front of several hundred supporters in downtown Sahuayo, Sánchez Gálvez urged voters "to throw out those responsible for the fact that there are 18 million Mexicans in the United States. The PRI sent them there. We want the people who have emigrated to the United States to return and find work here!" Neither of the two politicians has worked in the United States, though both have been there for vacations or business trips. Both Sánchez Gálvez and Ortiz support the right of Mexicans to vote abroad. According to Ortiz, "It's not right that we enjoy the resources that [migrants] send us, and we don't give them the vote." Because the PRD also supports extending suffrage to Mexicans abroad, Ortiz says it is only a question of time before an electoral reform bill passes the Mexican Congress. No party holds a majority in either chamber of the new Congress, but the PAN and PRD together would have the votes to pass such a bill. Neither Ortiz nor Sánchez Gálvez was aware of the proposal to create an extra-territorial congressional district for Mexicans abroad. Ortiz said he would view such a district favorably, noting that its representatives would be too few to affect voting significantly at the national level. "Mexicans abroad would never be the ones who would decide who governs and who doesn't govern." Ortiz said such a district would not be a politically viable proposal, however. Ninety-eight percent of Mexicans abroad live in the United States. A district created essentially in the United States would raise questions of national sovereignty and U.S. intervention.

In interviews, both politicians spoke very favorably of the participation of Sahuayans abroad in Mexican politics. According to Sánchez Gálvez, Sahuayans abroad do not owe anything to Sahuayo in a political or economic sense. "It is Sahuayo that owes them," he said. "Thanks to them, there is more commerce here and

---

[35] These results are unofficial.

[36] The *suplente* assumes the role of the deputy in the latter's absence.

in the region. If it were not for them and the money they send to their families, hundreds or thousands of jobs in the shoe shops and all the other businesses would not have the sales they do now. They wouldn't be rich without those people in the United States."

Panista leaders are politically poised to move beyond campaign rhetoric and create the legal conditions for migrants' fuller participation in their communities of origin. Without changes in Mexican law, migrants' access to political rights will be severely restricted, and even their indirect influence will likely be minimal. Similarly, the state's willingness to work with migrants, and vice versa, will determine the possibilities for cross-border philanthropic projects. In an era of transnational migration, the state continues to exercise tremendous influence over claims to all forms of citizenship. Yet, as the comments of the newly elected deputy and his suplente suggest, migrants' economic strength is closer than ever to creating access to direct political power.

CHAPTER 5

Comparative Organizational Models of Michoacano Migrants

The Jiquilpan Model: Institutionalizing Transnational Politics

Several politicians in Sahuayo have informally suggested establishing a sister-city relationship with Santa Ana, given that there is a large community of Sahuayans there who could act as a liaison. These leaders hope to emulate the success of municipal presidents in neighboring Jiquilpan (population 37,000) and Cojumatlán (population 11,000) who have worked with their respective Southern California satellite communities in Inglewood and South El Monte to create sister-city relationships.

In 1996, the PRD municipal president of Jiquilpan asked a friend in California to invite Jiquilpense migrants to a meeting in Inglewood. The municipal president, Francisco Mora, spoke to the group by speakerphone from Jiquilpan and encouraged them to form an organization of Jiquilpenses. The meeting led to the formation of the Association of Jiquilpenses Living in the United States.[37] Mora's later proposal to officials at Inglewood City Hall that Jiquilpan and Inglewood become sister cities was unsuccessful until the association contacted a Cuban-American Inglewood city council member who took an interest in the club. With the help of the city council member, the association and Mora negotiated a sister-city agreement in which the cities exchanged two delegations. During the Inglewood delegation's first visit to Jiquilpan, a Korean-American businessman accompanied them to look for investment opportunities (which never materialized). Inglewood also donated used fire-fighting equipment and computers to

---

[37] Unlike many other HTAs which grew out of hometown soccer clubs (Zabin and Escala Rabadán 1998, Massey et al. 1987), the Jiquilpan association has not cooperated with existing Jiquilpense soccer clubs that raise funds for local team expenses rather than projects for Jiquilpan.

Jiquilpan, but for over a year they have sat in storage in Inglewood because the proper import permits have not been arranged with Mexican customs. A student exchange program, which was part of the original agreement, has not yet been implemented either.

Nevertheless, the sister-city relationship carries real advantages for the association. The association now has access to Inglewood city resources such as the free use of city property for Jiquilpense art exhibitions, as well as the less tangible benefit of increased legitimacy through its interaction with Inglewood government officials. While the association does not officially endorse political candidates in the United States or Mexico, association members have campaigned for the reelection of the Cuban-American councilman. In general, there are weak links between Los Angeles Mexican hometown associations and California politicians (Zabin and Escala Rabadán 1998), but the case of Jiquilpan illustrates some of the potential benefits for the associations and political leaders in California.

The majority of the association leaders are long-term migrants, many of whom own homes and small businesses in California. Several of the most important leaders are women, unlike the exclusively male leadership of Sahuayan transnational organizations. One of the most active leaders is a homemaker who has lived in the United States for twenty-seven years. She returns to Jiquilpan once or twice a year, but she primarily lives in Inglewood so she can be closer to her three children, including one who serves in the U.S. army. "It's a shame that we go [north] for our kids, and because of our kids we don't return," she said. The current association president, who is the son of a former Jiquilpense municipal president and federal deputy, has a Master's degree in engineering from a Mexican university but has been unable to complete professional licensing requirements in California, where he has lived for the last ten years. He currently works as a bellhop at a hotel near the Los Angeles international airport. He returns to Jiquilpan twice a year. Participation in the association is a means to raise one's symbolic capital, not only in Jiquilpan but also among the community of Jiquilpenses living in California. Again, there is evidence that integration into life in the United States and transnationalism need not be mutually exclusive.

The Jiquilpan association has continued to maintain close ties with the municipal presidents of Jiquilpan. Mora made two trips to meet association members in Inglewood. The current PRI municipal president, who succeeded Mora, paid an official visit to Inglewood in 1999 accompanied by the priísta state deputy for the district that includes Jiquilpan and Sahuayo. The continuity of the association's relationship with the municipal presidency, despite a shift in party control, was an important milestone for the association and strengthened its affirmation of an apolitical agenda. The current municipal president, Juan Manuel Figueroa, says he supports the rights of Mexicans to vote abroad. When he worked in Chicago as a 22-year-old, he was impressed by the large parades of Mexicans on Mexican Independence Day. Mexicans in the United States "represent Mexico," he said, so they have the right to participate in Mexican politics (author interview 1999). Figueroa returned to Inglewood in November 1999 with two Jiquilpan city officials for the association's annual ball, at which he crowned the new Miss Jiquilpan USA.

The Miss Jiquilpan pageant encourages a sense of Jiquilpense identity among the second generation of immigrants, provides a spectacle to attract interest in the ball, and serves as the key fund-raising mechanism for the association. This is not a beauty pageant per se. For the first three years of the contest, the winner was chosen based on her ability to sell tickets. Candidates tended to be the daughters of established migrants who could afford to buy large numbers of tickets. There continues to be an unstated rule that candidates must have legal status in the United States, because the winner must travel to Jiquilpan to represent the norteños. Several undocumented women expressed interest in participating, but they were turned away by the association. In this case, the U.S. government indirectly limits transnational activities through its border controls.

The U.S.–born woman who in 1996 represented Jiquilpenses living in the United States flew to Jiquilpan to participate in the fiesta of the Mexican Revolution and to compete for the unified crown of Miss Jiquilpan by raising sponsorships. She competed against the Miss Jiquilpan elected in Jiquilpan and the Miss Jiquilpan elected by Jiquilpenses living in Mexico City. During the closing moments of the contest, the mother of the Inglewood candidate, who was also an association board member, pledged the $14,000 raised by the association to support her daughter. The Inglewood candidate handily trounced her competitors. This use of association funds was controversial in California and Jiquilpan, although the money was eventually used to renovate the public marketplace. Pledging the funds in a competition created the impression that the Jiquilpenses in California were unfairly throwing their economic weight around to "buy" the election of the queen. Any recognition of migrants' extra-territorial citizenship claims

Figure 10. Cover of the program for the 1999 annual ball of the Association of Jiquilpenses living in California, featuring a photograph of Miss Jiquilpan 1998

through patronage of the marketplace renovation was nullified by the divisive image created by the competition between representatives of norteños and Jiquilpan residents. In subsequent years, the Miss Jiquilpan elected in Inglewood has traveled to Jiquilpan as a representative of the norteños but no longer as a competitor to the queen elected in Jiquilpan.

Pageant rules changed in 1999 to emphasize the pageant's role as a means of constructing a Jiquilpense identity for young women born in the United States. Tickets to the event were sold at $25. A panel of judges selected the queen from four candidates based on their performance in several categories. Each candidate donned indigenous clothing and gave a speech about Jiquilpan, danced to a 1950s rock-and-roll hit in a fuzzy pink sweater and black capris, and answered questions about what it means to be Jiquilpense. Because Jiquilpan is a mestizo town, the young Jiquilpense women in Inglewood who dressed in hyper-indigenous clothing appeared to be more "native" than Jiquilpenses themselves. The young women's bodies became a locus for preserving notions of Jiquilpense "tradition," while at the same time their experience in the United States was acknowledged with North American music and the joint display of the U.S. and Mexican flags.

The 19-year-old winner was U.S. born but left when she was one year old to live in Jiquilpan. She returned to Southern California at age 15. Her speech about the history of Jiquilpan ended with a rousing _"Viva Jiquilpan!"_ that brought loud applause from the Jiquilpense delegation, which had sat impassively through the American-style dance routine. By making her membership claim in front of the delegation, the candidate's affirmation of membership was thrust into the transnational public discourse. Municipal President Figueroa confirmed her claim by publicly inviting her to Jiquilpan. He noted that the candidates and the association were working for the betterment of Jiquilpan, just as he was.

Shifting the emphasis of the pageant away from fund-raising is controversial within the club leadership, given that developing projects in Jiquilpan is its primary raison d'être. The funds raised in the first pageant were used to renovate the Jiquilpan public market. The following year, the association raised $5,000 for a childcare center. Representatives of the association handed over a check to the Jiquilpan municipal treasurer and videotaped the transaction in order to prove that the funds were delivered to the city as promised. The migrants' use of videotapes as a record of government transactions that can be played for contributors in the United States has been noted elsewhere as an example of a new technology creating greater accountability in transnational political practices (R. Smith 1995). Despite the confirming evidence of the videotape and receipts, rumors circulate in Jiquilpan and Inglewood that some of the funds were diverted for illicit purposes. While these allegations remain unproved, they have dampened the enthusiasm of Jiquilpenses in California to contribute to association fund-raising. All funds raised are now spent directly by the association when its board of directors visits Jiquilpan. In 1998 the association donated $3,000 worth of food and clothing to a home for indigent seniors, a drug rehabilitation clinic, and low-income Jiquilpenses selected by board family members living in Jiquilpan. Although the municipal president offered city resources such as a truck to deliver the donations, the municipality no longer controls the resources.

Jiquilpenses in California have been able to demand accountability in the distribution of resources they have collected in a way that would have been difficult had they lived in Jiquilpan. The migrants' ability to produce resources outside the territory controlled by the government, away from its coercive apparatus, has given migrants new leverage in their relationships with the state. Jiquilpenses abroad cannot force the government of Jiquilpan to become more accountable, but they can create incentives for greater government accountability through their ability to channel or restrict resources to public projects. Because the civic associations in the United States have no coercive capacity that can be used against potential donors, the HTAs are also bound to the same requirements of accountability. Migrants are only likely to succeed in carrying out projects in their communities of origin when there are mechanisms in place that create public trust in both the associations and the Mexican state.

El Granjenal: Building Infrastructure through Informal Networks

El Granjenal provides a dramatically different example of the way other Michoacano migrants organize. Not only do El Granjenal's migrants continue to take collective action for the village's benefit, but they have transformed it to the point that its infrastructure development is a model for the region. El Granjenal is an isolated mestizo village in the hills an hour's drive from the nearest paved road in the northeastern municipio of Puruándiro. For eleven months of the year, it is populated almost exclusively by women,

Figure 11. A hairdresser in Santa Ana, California, advertises his services on the wall of a bullring in El Granjenal sponsored by migrants (*photo by David Fitzgerald*)

Figure 12. At right, Salvador Arceo, 61, shouts during a 2000 PAN campaign rally in the central plaza of Sahuayo. Arceo has been migrating back and forth from Sahuayo to the United States since 1961. He is a sometime resident of Costa Mesa, where his wife and seven children still live (*photo by David Fitzgerald*)

children, and the elderly.[38] Young teenagers roller-blade past retired braceros on streets lined with crumbling adobe houses and empty two-story vacation homes crowned by satellite dishes and perhaps even a rooftop basketball court. In December, the houses are briefly occupied by returning migrants who double the village's population during the fiesta of the Virgin of Guadalupe. Although fewer migrants returned in the early 1990s, in the last few years there has been a dramatic increase in returnees as migrants who have legalized their status can return to El Granjenal without worrying about crossing back to the United States illegally once their vacation is over.

Growing corn or beans on the surrounding ejido land is a money-losing proposition, so the town is utterly dependent on remittances. "Here the village relies on California," said a 50-year-old retired construction worker who first went to California as a 17-year-old without legal papers. Now he is an amnestied U.S. green-card holder and Mexican citizen. He enjoys life at his house in El Granjenal with three of his children (two of whom were born in California) or at his house in Santa Ana with his remaining children, who were born in El Granjenal. He travels back and forth several times a year, living off the remittances of his sons or occasionally working a few shifts in Santa Ana.

Even the political structure of El Granjenal has been transplanted 2,400 kilometers to a "satellite community" in Santa Ana which is bigger than the community of origin. The construction worker described above is the *encargado del orden*.[39] His 61-year-old suplente is a former bracero who arranged his permanent residency documents in 1962 and works in construction in Santa Ana. Like the encargado del orden, he has a house and children in both Santa Ana and El Granjenal. The dual leadership structure allows one of the encargados to travel to Santa Ana to work or visit family while the other minds the affairs of El Granjenal. Both men travel back and forth across the border several times a year, shifting their class identities between economically successful elected officials in El Granjenal and working-class migrants in Santa Ana.

---

[38] The 1990 INEGI census lists a population of 1,006, which includes all absent migrants with a spouse in the village (INEGI 1991). The *Los Angeles Times* estimated there were 3,000 people from El Granjenal in Santa Ana in 1997 (Cleeland 1997).

[39] The *encargado del orden* is the highest-ranking official in the village. He is elected by an assembly of household heads to maintain order and act as the liaison with the municipio government.

The election of two leaders to a position helps Mexicans in small communities throughout the region fulfill their community obligations without forcing them into the financial hardship of restricting their migration. The dual election system predates the beginning of mass international migration, but it serves a useful contemporary function in balancing the political needs of a community with the economic interests of its leaders.

Public works in El Granjenal—such as road paving and the installation of drainage systems—are accomplished through the faena system of community labor. For example, if the village assembly decides to pave a street, the household head from each house on the street is responsible for donating labor or money to the project. Many of the houses are unoccupied for most of the year because their owners are in California, but the absent owners remain responsible for contributing to the faena. Absent owners must send money to family members in El Granjenal to contract a day laborer to fulfill their duty. Returning migrants who have not fulfilled their duty are asked to compensate by performing other faenas. Although village leaders claim that compliance is universal because of social pressure and the migrants' goodwill, in a 1999 public assembly to discuss works projects, one angry resident claimed that the norteños do not complete their faenas. At the same assembly, the visiting municipal president of Puruándiro congratulated El Granjenal for its developed infrastructure and noted that migrants are largely responsible. In a 1989 survey, 72 percent of residents said migration had helped the town more than the government had (López Castro and Barkin 1990).

Public assemblies in El Granjenal elect committee members to organize public projects. The committee members then select members of a fund-raising committee in Santa Ana. The members of the Santa Ana committee do not know they have been selected until after the fact.[40] Migrants vacationing in El Granjenal return to Santa Ana with letters of appointment that they give to designated committee members. The positions are rotated each year to prevent the same group of migrants from repeatedly shouldering the organizational and financial burden. Most of the committee members in Santa Ana are well-established men with their own small businesses or steady jobs. Indeed, most migrants from El Granjenal have legal status and have prospered in the United States, in

---

[40] The election of absent persons is not restricted to migrants. The current president of the _comisariado ejidal_ (ejido commission) was elected by an assembly he did not attend.

part because of their affiliation with the union Labor Hall in Santa Ana, which for the last thirty years has provided hundreds of migrants with well-paying jobs in the construction industry (Cleeland 1997).

The transnational committees work along parallel, mutually exclusive lines. For example, the street-paving committee operates independently of the committee raising funds for the fiesta of the Virgin. Each committee holds fund-raising parties or solicits money door-to-door within personal networks. In 1998 the fiesta committee in Santa Ana raised $20,000. When a migrant based in Santa Ana initiates a project for El Granjenal, no fund-raising can begin until the encargado del orden approves the project. For example, a 25-year-old Santa Ana resident who was born in California but spent half his life in El Granjenal is developing a soccer field in El Granjenal. He waited three months to receive a document of approval with the official seal of the encargado del orden before organizing a soccer tournament and other activities that raised $2,000 for the project.

The Labor Hall in Santa Ana independently sponsors an annual dance that raises funds for projects in El Granjenal. There is also a Club Guadalupano in Santa Ana with a rotating five-person membership that raises money for projects such as a *plaza de toros* (bullring) that has been under construction for ten years and is now almost complete. Patrons place ads on the sides of the bullring advertising the telephone numbers and addresses of businesses such as hairdressers and gardening services 2,400 kilometers away. Migrants have also raised money for church renovations and for the construction of the kinds of facilities they have come to expect while living in the North, like church restrooms and comfortable pews. Priests traveling to Santa Ana have been important actors in maintaining a sense of community among El Granjenal migrants. El Granjenal migrants have participated in every recent village construction project—from a jail to a water tank—even though the migrants are not formally organized or associated with the Mexican consulate, municipal government, or other state agencies.

Bringing the Local Back In: Comparing Three Transnational Communities

One Sahuayan community leader in Santa Ana familiar with the many projects of El Granjenal migrants asked, "Why can't we do that?" Clearly, the El Granjenal experience arises from a far different milieu than that of Sahuayo. Sahuayo is a large town extremely well integrated into the regional economy, less economically dependent on migration, and without a tradition of faena (although Sahuayan neighbors do cooperate with the municipio to pave the streets in front of their homes). Sahuayan migrants are also much more dispersed in the United States than migrants from El Granjenal, who have concentrated in Santa Ana and the "occupational niches" of construction work and gardening (see Waldinger and Bozorgmehr 1996). The union hiring hall continues to play a central social and economic role in the El Granjenal satellite community.

Rivera Salgado argues that the literature on transnational migrant politics has paid too little attention to the particular histories of sending and receiving communities (1999). The difference between the organizational strategies of migrants from Jiquilpan and Sahuayo is particularly striking because of the towns' proximity (10 kilometers), rough similarity in size (37,000 in Jiquilpan compared to 60,000 in Sahuayo), and similar migration histories and destinations. Local histories may provide an explanation. As detailed at the beginning of chapter 4, Sahuayo has long fostered an identity as Catholic, conservative, and anti-government. During the Mexican Revolution, Jiquilpan was maderista while Sahuayo defended the regime and became known as "Porfirio Díaz's Sahuayo." The antagonism between Sahuayo and Jiquilpan was greatly exacerbated by the cardenista Agrarian Reform and the widespread perception that lingers in Jiquilpan and Sahuayo that the Cárdenas clan deliberately steered transportation routes, government offices, and cultural institutions away from Sahuayo and toward Jiquilpan (Vargas González 1993). Even today, Sahuayans complain that the government handed Jiquilpan everything—from a university to lush landscaped trees—while Sahuayo has been forced to rely on its own pluck.

Although Sahuayo has become the economic hegemon of the Ciénega de Chapala, Jiquilpan continues to dominate regional politics (Zepeda Patterson 1989). Jiquilpan is the seat of the regional congressional district and has more state and federal government offices despite its smaller size. In the last few years, Sahuayo has become more politically powerful, but the legacy of anti-government sentiment may explain why Sahuayan migrants have generally avoided an institutionalized relationship with Mexican state organs at any level, in contrast to a long history of migrant affiliation with the Church. Conversely, the Church-migrant relationship in Jiquilpan is relatively weak, notwithstanding the visit of a Jiquilpense priest to Inglewood in 1999, while the HTA–municipio and HTA–consular relationships remain quite strong.

Different settlement patterns in the United States also affect the formation of transnational associations. Jiquilpenses in the United States are not as geographically or economically concentrated as are migrants from El Granjenal, but they are much more concentrated than Sahuayans. Jiquilpenses have been working in the service industry in areas around Los Angeles International Airport, like Lennox and Inglewood, since the 1960s (McDonnell 1995). It may be easier for Jiquilpenses to organize because they are from a town that has benefited from a close relationship with the government and because they are more concentrated in the United States. Only case studies rooted in particular translocal histories can tease out the variables that affect forms of association and transnational negotiations of citizenship.

Each organizational model carries advantages and disadvantages. In the Sahuayan model, there are multiple transnational networks with low levels of institutionalization and no relationship with the Mexican consulate (with the exception of the Colonia Sahuayense in Chicago). The advantage of such a model has been that the consulate cannot intervene in the selection of migrant leaders or co-opt migrant organizations into the PRI apparatus. Migrant organizations can convincingly maintain a nonpartisan stance that attracts migrants alienated by partisan politics. Working with civil society in Mexico rather than with state and local governments also prevents the distribution of funds in a clientelistic fashion that serves the interests of politicians.

As the examples of the Cruz Ambar and the Sahuayan hospital delegation demonstrate, however, it is difficult for a private organization to move goods across the border without the cooperation of Mexican authorities. A working relationship with the consulate could ease bureaucratic paperwork, lend "official" legitimacy to the organization, introduce the group to like-minded organizations, and offer comparative perspectives based on the experience of other migrant associations. With the election of Vicente Fox, who represents not only an alternate political party but a party that does not have the massive machinery of the PRI, consulates are less likely to act, or appear to act, as mere extensions of the party in power. As long as the consulates do not appear to become panista organs, consular affiliation is increasingly likely to offer HTAs organizational advantages without risking a loss of autonomy. A more recent strategy is to organize the HTAs into an autonomous federation. HTA club presidents in Los Angeles—from Zacatecas, Jalisco, Guanajuato, Oaxaca, and Sinaloa—organized a federation in June 2000 with the help of union leaders (Cleeland 2000). The organization should be able to strengthen the collective power of HTAs vis-à-vis the consulate and lobby more effectively for a new amnesty for illegal immigrants.

Working outside the consular framework is no guarantee of democratic procedures or accountability, of course. The history of the Colonia Sahuayense illustrates the dangers of internal corruption that threatens the long-term health of the group. Institutionalized arrangements such as elected officers and bookkeeping could minimize the misuse of funds. The plurality of informal networks may encourage the participation of a wide range of migrants with diverse interests, but the organizational efforts of one network may be stymied by charges of corruption in another. When one Sahuayan network is tainted by charges of misuse of funds, participation in transnational activities declines on a community-wide level. Further, the absence of a central Sahuayan HTA dilutes the potential collective power of migrants in their interactions with other institutions such as the U.S. or Mexican governments.

The Jiquilpan HTA demonstrates the potential advantages of a central association that cooperates with local U.S. authorities and Mexican officials at the municipal and consular levels. Because the Jiquilpense community in Southern California has a single unified association, Jiquilpense migrants have increased clout with municipal officials in Jiquilpan and Inglewood. One potential political strength of transnational migrants is their ability to mediate between different cultures, languages, and even political systems. The sister-city relationship brokered by the Jiquilpense HTA has not achieved its full potential, but it suggests a useful model.

The village of El Granjenal is less easily compared with large towns like Sahuayo and Jiquilpan, but the transnational practices of El Granjenal's migrants demonstrate that formal institutions are not always necessary to channel effective action. Without romanticizing the value of *gemeinschaft*, it seems that the transnational community of a village and its concentrated migrants is likely to encourage the thick social networks and trust that permit effective organizing even in the absence of formal institutions. When participation and contributions are voluntary, high levels of social capital encourage accountability.

Because migrants have placed themselves outside the boundaries of the state, they do not have enforceable obligations toward the state or its subnational units. Government attempts to enlist the voluntary aid of migrants are unlikely to succeed unless they can offer migrants confidence in the accountability and transparency of the system. Similarly, migrants are not obliged to give their time or money to religious or civic transnational networks. Migrants no longer support these networks when they lose confidence. While migrants' refusal to cooperate may prevent sustained fraud, it is a limited strategy for resistance. Rather than searching for creative ways to develop projects in Sahuayo transparently and efficiently, a much more common response among Sahuayan migrants is to withdraw from transnational collective action altogether. In the absence of such participation, migrants' claims to extra-territorial citizenship become even more tenuous.

CHAPTER 6

Conclusion

In their prescription for a research agenda for the study of transnational migration, Portes et al. divide transnational activities into a typology of economic, political, and sociocultural practices (1999). While such distinctions may be useful, it is also important to consider the interactions between different kinds of practices. Studying citizenship as a process rather than a fixed status allows me to show the linkages between cultural identity, behavioral norms, economic activity, and political negotiations. Extraterritorial citizenship cannot be understood if it is only studied using a narrow definition of politics. The debate over the extension of suffrage to Mexicans abroad is an easily recognized form of extra-territorial citizenship negotiation, but an analysis of transnational communities reveals more subtle processes. A model of citizenship like the one I have proposed here helps explain the social interactions that are the basis of transnational politics on multiple levels.

"Transnationalism" as it is used here is not some vague nostalgia for the homeland, but rather a set of concrete, observable practices where migrants actively assert their claims to membership in their communities of origin. Not all Sahuayan migrants live transnational lives. Many leave Sahuayo and never return. For others, the occasional return vacation or telephone call does not reach the level of intensity shown by the migrants described in this study. Strikingly, some of the most transnationally active Sahuayans are those who bear multiple markers of permanent U.S. settlement, such as home and business ownership in the United States, permanent resident legal status, and even U.S. naturalization.

Although there is evidence of U.S.–born immigrant children participating in transnational activities such as the Miss Jiquilpan pageant, it is unlikely that strong transnational connections will remain by the third generation. The generational argument should not be used to preclude the study of transnationalism, however. Even if transnational practices are only widely found in the first generation of immigrants, the share of foreign-born among the Mexican-origin population of greater Los Angeles rose from 25 percent in 1970 to 46 percent in 1990 (Waldinger and Bozorgmehr 1996). There are an estimated 120 million recent international immigrants (Castles and Miller 1998), and many of them will continue to actively maintain and create ties to their places of origin. The impact of those ties is particularly dramatic when viewed from the perspective of the places of origin. A few thousand dollars raised at a party may seem inconsequential from a U.S. perspective, but an ambulance or a water tank in Michoacán purchased with that money can make an important difference in the daily lives of sending community residents and those who seek inclusion in the community.

The present work does not intend to celebrate extra-territorial citizenship as a principle. Opponents of extra-territorial citizenship may have their own political interests in mind, but they raise theoretically valid concerns about a model of citizenship that emphasizes rights over obligations, passive entitlements, and the assertion of an interest in the public space without a daily presence. There is a tension between a reconceptualization of the polis as the transnational public space of the imagined community and the assertion that the polis should still be defined as a geographic space where citizens live together.

The representation of Sahuayans abroad as a corporate group led by a few individuals is also problematic on a theoretical level. Bendix describes the conflicting principles of plebiscitarianism and functionalism. In the plebiscitarian model, the individual has a direct relationship with the state. The rights and duties of the individual are paramount. In the functional model, corporate groups mediate between the individual and the state. Corporate groups have rights and obligations, but these rights always come at the expense of the individual (Bendix 1977). Informants in Sahuayo, Jiquilpan, and El Granjenal did not express this tension, perhaps because Mexican politics has been organized along corporate lines since the founding of the PRI. Nevertheless, the corporate organization of migrants raises questions about direct democratic representation in transnational political practices.

The negotiation of moral forms of extra-territorial citizenship in communities of towns and villages is informed by the same principles that are evident in the negotiation of legal extra-territorial citizenship on the national level. The transnational economy and politics are inextricably linked. Appeals to migrants to invest in Mexico and to maintain a high volume of remittances open spaces for migrants to demand political rights such as absentee voting. Migrant assertions of Mexican identity are part of this debate. Some Mexicans who reject extra-territorial citizenship charge that migrants are pochos or traitors who do not deserve to participate in Mexican politics.

Even when Sahuayan migrants do contribute economically to Sahuayo through philanthropies, private investment, remittances, or collective projects, they may have difficulty making sustainable claims to extra-territorial citizenship. Evidence from Sahuayo and Jiquilpan demonstrates that displays of economic wealth can actually undermine claims to citizenship rights by suggesting values corrupted by exposure to the foreign culture of the United States. The perceived link between migrants and immoral behavior— from throwing ostentatious parties to painting gang logos—makes it very difficult for Sahuayan migrants to successfully assert a citizenship that is primarily moral. Claims to extra-territorial citizenship are only likely to be recognized when economic participation is accompanied by displays of a common cultural identity. The significance of culture and its expression through public displays and subscription to behavioral norms suggests that religious institutions will continue to play a major role in transnational politics at the local level, particularly in conservative towns like Sahuayo. Public projects that build migrants' collective symbolic capital become increasingly important in the face of resistance to their recognition as good members of the community.

Recent developments on the national level may have important impacts in the negotiation of extra-territorial citizenship in every sense. Vicente Fox has promised that as president he will extend suffrage in Mexican presidential elections to Mexican citizens living abroad. Together, the PAN and the PRD have the votes in both houses of Congress to pass such legislation. Although technical details and the question of who exactly will be considered a Mexican citizen remain unresolved, the vote abroad appears to be close to realization, at least for Mexican citizens with the IFE voting credential. The establishment of the legal principle of extra-territorial citizenship with full political rights would give weight to the moral claims to extra-territorial citizenship on the local level. Once the political rights of Mexicans outside the country are publicly recognized, it would be difficult to retract that recognition and shift the public discourse back to a denigration of norteños as gringo-ized Mexicans. Until now, it has been easy for those who reject extra-territorial citizenship to point to the minimal influence of migrants on elections as evidence that migrants have lost interest in Mexico and no longer deserve its protection.

The U.S. campaigns of candidates like Vicente Fox and Cuauhtémoc Cárdenas appear to have had little direct impact on the 2000 election. This is partially because of the high barriers to participation, such as the inability to vote from abroad, the strictly limited number of ballots at the special polling sites on the Mexican border, and the long waiting times for an IFE credential. Removing some of the barriers to participation would finally reveal the extent to which migrants want to engage in transnational politics. Evidence from Sahuayo suggests that U.S.–based migrants from a PAN stronghold did little to influence the 2000 elections by calling their friends or family in Sahuayo. Only those migrants who live truly transnational lives and were in Sahuayo during the elections participated actively.

Does the failure of Sahuayans in the United States to respond to the campaign pleas of Fox and Cárdenas suggest that the candidates were wasting their time? Trips to the United States by Mexican political candidates and elected officials have multiple and diverse objectives. These objectives extend beyond attempts to influence the vote directly or indirectly. In the case of Fox, his U.S. campaign tour seemed less an overture to migrants than an opportunity to demonstrate to the U.S. government and influential sectors that, if elected president, he would continue close relations with the United States. Even more importantly, Fox sought to demonstrate to the public in Mexico that he was "presidential material," capable of managing foreign policy, an important quality for the first opposition president in seventy-one years. Fox's rallies with Mexican migrants could be interpreted to a certain extent as a cover to avoid the image that he went to California as a supplicant before the U.S. government. In fact, the PRI attacked Fox on precisely these grounds and aired campaign advertisements accusing Fox of telling the U.S. media that Mexico should train its people to work as laborers in the United States.

Even when local Mexican officials encourage transnational community projects by traveling to the North, their greatest aim may not be promoting such projects so much as encouraging loyalty to the home community that will translate into family remittances and economic investment. The act of sponsoring a project or participating in a procession creates a sense of community identity. One municipal president in the Ciénega region noted that the municipio budget is far greater than any group remittances would ever be. Towns like Sahuayo do not need several thousand dollars to erect a statue in the plaza to honor migrants, but they desperately need the millions of dollars in remittances that drive local economies. Politicians of all parties hope that such projects will encourage migrants to feel like members of the community and respond with remittances and direct economic investment. The extent to which a new government can create the economic conditions that would encourage investment from U.S.–based migrants will have important implications for the negotiation of extraterritorial citizenship. If migrants respond with substantial investment, not only will they strengthen their claims to citizenship, but they will also likely demand increased rights to protect their material interests.

References

Alarcón, Rafael. 1986. "Los primeros norteños de Chavinda," *Relaciones* 3: 163–86.

———. 1988. "El proceso de 'norteñización': impacto de la migración internacional en Chavinda, Michoacán." In *Movimientos de población en el occidente de México,* edited by Thomas Calvo and Gustavo López. Zamora: El Colegio de Michoacán.

Anderson, Benedict. 1991. *Imagined Communities.* London: Verso.

Anderson, John Ward. 2000. "Politicians without Borders: Mexico's Candidates Court Support of Migrants in U.S.," *Washington Post,* May 9.

Appadurai, Arjun. 1991. "Global Ethnoscapes: Notes and Queries for a Transnational Anthropology." In *Recapturing Anthropology,* edited by R. Fox. Santa Fe, N.M.: School of American Research.

Austin, J. L. 1975. *How To Do Things with Words,* edited by J. O. Urmson and Marina Sbisa. Oxford: Clarendon.

Balderrama, Francisco E. 1982. *In Defense of La Raza: The Los Angeles Mexican Consulate and the Mexican Community, 1929 to 1936.* Tucson: University of Arizona Press.

Balibar, Etienne. 1988. "Propositions on Citizenship," *Ethics* 98: 723–30.

Basch, Linda, Nina Glick Schiller, and Cristina Szanton Blanc. 1994. *Nations Unbound: Transnational Projects, Postcolonial Predicaments and Deterritorialized Nation-States.* Langhorne, Penn.: Gordon and Breach.

Bendix, Reinhard. 1977. *Nation-Building and Citizenship.* Berkeley: University of California Press.

Binational Study on Migration between Mexico and the United States. 1997. Commission on Immigration Reform, U.S.A./Secretaría de Relaciones Exteriores, Mexico. Mexico City: Regina de los Ángeles.

Bourdieu, Pierre. 1986. "The Forms of Capital." In *Handbook of Theory and Research for the Sociology of Education,* edited by John G. Richardson. New York: Greenwood.

Brubaker, Rogers. 1989. "Citizenship and Naturalization: Policies and Politics." In *Immigration and the Politics of Citizenship in Europe and North America,* edited by Rogers Brubaker. New York: University Press of America.

————. 1992. *Citizenship and Nationhood in France and Germany*. Cambridge, Mass.: Harvard University Press.

Bruhn, Kathleen. 1999. "PRD Local Governments in Michoacán: Implications for Mexico's Democratization Process." In *Subnational Politics and Democratization in Mexico*, edited by Wayne A. Cornelius, Todd A. Eisenstadt, and Jane Hindley. La Jolla: Center for U.S.–Mexican Studies, University of California, San Diego.

Bustamante, Jorge A. 1986. "Chicano-Mexicano Relations from Practice to Theory." In *Chicano-Mexicano Relations*, edited by Tatcho Mindiola, Jr. and Max Martínez. Mexican American Studies Monograph, no. 4. Houston: Mexican American Studies Program, University of Houston, University Park.

Carens, Joseph. 1989. "Membership and Morality: Admission to Citizenship in Liberal Democratic States." In *Immigration and the Politics of Citizenship in Europe and North America*, edited by Rogers Brubaker. New York: University Press of America.

Castañeda, Jorge. 1993. "Mexico and California: The Paradox of Tolerance and Dedemocratization." In *The California-Mexico Connection*, edited by Abraham Lowenthal and Katrina Burgess. Stanford, Calif.: Stanford University Press.

Castles, Stephen, and Mark J. Miller. 1998. *The Age of Migration*. New York: Guilford.

Center for Demographic Research. 1999. California State University, Fullerton. On-line. http://cdr1.fullerton.edu.

Claiborne, William. 2000. "3 Expatriates Appear to Lose Congress Bids," *The Washington Post*, July 4.

Cleeland, Nancy. 1997. "Mexican Town Left Behind," *Los Angeles Times*, August 3.

————. 2000. "Mexican 'Hometown Clubs' Turn Activist," *Los Angeles Times*, June 8.

Clifford, James. 1994. "Diasporas," *Cultural Anthropology* 9 (3): 302–38.

Cornelius, Wayne A. 1990. "Labor Migration to the United States: Development Outcomes and Alternatives in Mexican Sending Communities." Final report to the Commission for the Study of International Migration and Cooperative Economic Development on research conducted under contract by the Center for U.S.–Mexican Studies, University of California, San Diego.

————. 1998a. "Ejido Reform: Stimulus or Alternative to Migration?" In *The Transformation of Rural Mexico: Reforming the Ejido Sector*, edited by Wayne A. Cornelius and David Myhre. La Jolla: Center for U.S.–Mexican Studies, University of California, San Diego.

——. 1998b. "The Structural Embeddedness of Demand for Mexican Immigrant Labor: New Evidence from California." In *Crossings: Mexican Immigration in Interdisciplinary Perspectives*, edited by Marcelo M. Suárez-Orozco. Cambridge, Mass.: David Rockefeller Center, Harvard University.

Cornelius, Wayne A., Ann L. Craig, and Jonathan Fox, eds. 1994. *Transforming State-Society Relations in Mexico: The National Solidarity Strategy*. La Jolla: Center for U.S.–Mexican Studies, University of California, San Diego.

Cornelius, Wayne A., and David Myhre, eds. 1998. *The Transformation of Rural Mexico: Reforming the Ejido Sector*. La Jolla: Center for U.S.–Mexican Studies, University of California, San Diego.

Craig, Ann L. 1983. *The First Agraristas: An Oral History of a Mexican Agrarian Reform Movement*. Berkeley: University of California Press.

Darling, Juanita. 1993. "Migrants' Social, Economic Ties to Mexico Stay Strong," *Los Angeles Times*, November 29.

Das Gupta, Monisha. 1997. "'What Is Indian About You?' A Gendered Transnational Approach to Ethnicity," *Gender and Society* 2 (5): 572–96.

Dillon, Sam. 1998. "Mexico Weighs Voting by Its Emigrants in U.S.," *New York Times*, December 7.

Dinerman, Ina. 1982. *Migrants and Stay-at-Homes: A Comparative Study of Rural Migration from Michoacán, Mexico*. Monograph Series, no. 5. La Jolla: Center for U.S.–Mexican Studies, University of California, San Diego.

Dresser, Denise. 1993. "Exporting Conflict: Transboundary Consequences of Mexican Politics." In *The California-Mexico Connection*, edited by Abraham Lowenthal and Katrina Burgess. Stanford, Calif.: Stanford University Press.

Durand, Jorge. 1994. *Más allá de la línea: patrones migratorios entre México y Estados Unidos*. Mexico City: Consejo Nacional para la Cultura y las Artes.

Escala Rabadán, Luis. 1999. "Political Empowerment, Immigrant Communities and Their Organizations: Mexican Hometown Associations in Los Angeles, California." Paper presented at the University of California Comparative Immigration and Integration Program Research Workshop, Center for U.S.–Mexican Studies, University of California, San Diego, February 19.

Espinosa, Víctor. 1999. "La Federación de Clubes Michoacanos en Illinois: construyendo puentes entre Chicago y Michoacán." Chicago: Heartland Alliance for Human Needs and Human Rights.

Félix, Edgar. 1999a. "Zacatecas, estado transfronterizo," *El Financiero*, January 15.

———. 1999b. "La suave patria y Estados Unidos," *El Financiero*, January 13.

Foerster, Robert F. 1919. *The Italian Emigration of Our Times*. Cambridge, Mass.: Harvard University Press.

Fonseca, Omar. 1988. "De Jaripo a Stockton, California: un caso de migración en Michoacán." In *Movimientos de población en el occidente de México*, edited by Thomas Calvo and Gustavo López. Zamora: El Colegio de Michoacán.

Forbes Adams, Victoria. 1994. "Profit and Tradition in Rural Manufacture: Sandal Production in Sahuayo, Michoacán, Mexico." Ph.D. dissertation, University College London.

Foucault, Michel. 1969. *The Archaeology of Knowledge*. New York: Pantheon.

Fox, Ben. 2000. "Mexicans Head South to Cast Ballots," Associated Press, July 3.

Gamio, Manuel. 1969. *Mexican Immigration to the United States: A Study of Human Migration and Adjustment*. New York: Arno.

Gans, Herbert J. 1979. "Symbolic Ethnicity: The Future of Ethnic Groups and Cultures in America," *Ethnic and Racial Studies* 2 (1): 1–20.

Gellner, Ernest. 1983. *Nations and Nationalism*. Ithaca, N.Y.: Cornell University Press.

Gledhill, John. 1993. *Casi nada: capitalismo, estado y los campesinos de Guaracha*. Zamora: El Colegio de Michoacán.

———. 1995. *Neoliberalism, Transnationalization, and Rural Poverty: A Case Study of Michoacán, Mexico*. Boulder, Colo.: Westview.

Glick Schiller, Nina. 1999. "Who Are These Guys? A Transnational Reading of the U.S. Immigrant Experience." In *Identities on the Move: Transnational Processes in North America and the Caribbean Basin*, edited by Liliana R. Goldin. Studies on Culture and Society, vol. 7. Albany, N.Y.: Institute for Mesoamerican Studies, University of Albany.

Glick Schiller, Nina, Linda Basch, and Cristina Blanc-Szanton, eds. 1992. *Towards a Transnational Perspective on Migration: Race, Class, Ethnicity and Nationalism Reconsidered*. New York: New York Academy of Sciences.

Glick Schiller, Nina, and Georges E. Fouron. 1999. "Terrains of Blood and Nation: Haitian Transnational Social Fields," *Ethnic and Racial Studies* 22 (2): 340–65.

Godines, Valeria. 1999. "O.C. Catholic Churches Look to Mexico to Help Supply Priests," *Orange County Register*, August 31.

Goldberg, Barry. 1992. "Historical Reflections on Transnationalism, Race, and the American Immigrant Saga." In *Towards a Transnational Perspective on Migration: Race, Class, Ethnicity and Nationalism Reconsidered*, edited by Nina Glick Schiller, Linda Basch, and Cristina Blanc-Szanton. New York: New York Academy of Sciences.

Goldring, Luin. 1996. "Blurring Borders: Constructing Transnational Community in the Process of Mexico–U.S. Migration," *Research in Community Sociology* 6: 69–104.

———. 1998. "The Power of Status in Transnational Social Fields," *Comparative Urban and Community Research* 6: 165–95.

———. 1999. "El Estado mexicano y las organizaciones transmigrantes. ¿Reconfigurando la nación y las relaciones entre estado y sociedad civil?" In *Fronteras fragmentadas*, edited by Gail Mummert. Zamora: El Colegio de Michoacán.

Gómez-Quiñones, Juan. 1973. "Piedras Contra La Luna. México en Aztlán y Aztlán en México: Chicano-Mexicano Relations and the Mexican Consulates, 1900–1920, An Extended Research Note." Paper presented at the IV International Congress of Mexican Studies, Santa Monica, California, October.

González, Luis. 1979. *Sahuayo*. Monografías Municipales del Estado de Michoacán. Morelia: Gobierno del Estado de Michoacán.

González Baker, Susan, Frank D. Bean, Agustín Escobar Latapí, and Sidney Weintraub. 1998. "U.S. Immigration Policies and Trends: The Growing Importance of Migration from Mexico." In *Crossings: Mexican Immigration in Interdisciplinary Perspectives*, edited by Marcelo M. Suárez-Orozco. Cambridge, Mass.: David Rockefeller Center, Harvard University.

González Gutiérrez, Carlos. 1995. "La organización de los inmigrantes mexicanos en Los Angeles: la lealtad de los oriundos," *Revista Mexicana de Política Exterior* 46: 59–101.

Guarnizo, Luis Eduardo. 1998. "The Rise of Transnational Social Formations: Mexican and Dominican Responses to Transnational Migration," *Political Power and Social Theory* 12: 45–94.

Guarnizo, Luis Eduardo, Arturo Ignacio Sánchez, and Elizabeth M. Roach. 1999. "Mistrust, Fragmented Solidarity, and Trans-national Migration: Colombians in New York City and Los Angeles," *Ethnic and Racial Studies* 22 (2): 367–96.

Guerrero, Juan Antonio. 1998. "Chicanos y mecsicanos," *Guía*, April 19.

Gurza, Teresa. 1998. "Urgente, definir política para emigrantes," *Crónica*, April 1.

Gutiérrez, Armando. 1986. "The Chicano Elite in Chicano-Mexicano Relations." In *Chicano-Mexicano Relations*, edited by Tatcho Mindiola, Jr., and Max Martínez. Mexican American Studies Monograph No. 4. Houston: Mexican American Studies Program, University of Houston, University Park.

Hammar, Tomas. 1989. "State, Nation, and Dual Citizenship." In *Immigration and the Politics of Citizenship in Europe and North America*, edited by Rogers Brubaker. New York: University Press of America.

Hernández Madrid, Miguel J. 1988. "Migración, estrategias de vida y concentración del poder político en un ejido de la región zamorana en Michoacán." In *Movimientos de población en el occidente de México*, edited by Thomas Calvo and Gustavo López. Zamora: El Colegio de Michoacán.

———. 1999. "Iglesias sin fronteras. Migrantes y conversos religiosos: cambios de identidad cultural en el noroeste de Michoacán." In *Fronteras fragmentadas*, edited by Gail Mummert. Zamora: El Colegio de Michoacán.

Hernández Santiago, Joel. 1985. "Tlazazalca, país de golondrinos," *Relaciones* 23: 61–69.

Hispanic Databook of U.S. Cities and Counties. 1994. Milpitas, Calif.: Toucan Valley Publications.

Hobsbawm, Eric J. 1990. *Nations and Nationalism since 1780: Programme, Myth and Reality.* New York: Cambridge University Press.

Holston, James. n.d.1. "Urban Citizenship and Globalization." In *Global City-Regions*, edited by Allen J. Scott. New York: Oxford University Press. Forthcoming.

———. n.d.2. "Citizenship in Uncivil Democracies." In *Unsettling Citizenship: Disjunctions of Democracy and Modernity.* Forthcoming.

Honig, Bonnie. 1998. "Immigrant America? How Foreignness 'Solves' Democracy's Problems," *Social Text* 56 (16) 3: 1–27.

IFE (Instituto Federal Electoral). 2000a. On-line. http://www.ife.org. mx/.

———. 2000b. *Atlas Electoral Federal de México, 1991–1997.* Mexico City: IFE.

INEGI (Instituto Nacional de Estadística, Geografía e Informática). 1991. *Michoacán. Resultados Definitivos Datos por Localidad. XI Censo General de Población y Vivienda, 1990.* Aguascalientes: INEGI.

———. 1997. *Perspectiva Estadística de Michoacán.* Aguascalientes: INEGI.

———. 1998. *Anuario Estadístico del Estado de Michoacán.* Aguascalientes: INEGI.

Iszaevich, Abraham. 1988. "Migración campesina del valle de Oaxaca." In *Migración en el Occidente de México*, edited by Gustavo López Castro. Zamora: El Colegio de Michoacán.

Jacobson, Matthew Frye. 1995. *Special Sorrows: The Diasporic Imagination of Irish, Polish, and Jewish Immigrants in the United States*. Cambridge, Mass.: Harvard University Press.

Jones, Richard C. 1995. *Ambivalent Journey: U.S. Migration and Economic Mobility in North-Central Mexico*. Tucson: University of Arizona Press.

Kearney, Michael. 1991. "Borders and Boundaries of State and Self at the End of Empire," *Journal of Historical Sociology* 4 (1): 52–74.

Kymlicka, Will. 1995. *Multicultural Citizenship*. Oxford: Oxford University Press.

La Jornada. 1999. "México: PRI boicotea debate de reforma electoral en el Senado," July 1.

Leftwich, Adrian. 1983. *Redefining Politics: People, Resources and Power*. London: Methuen.

Levitt, Peggy. 1998. "Social Remittances: Migration-Driven, Local-Level Forms of Cultural Diffusion," *International Migration Review*, Fall, pp. 926–48.

———. 1999. "Towards an Understanding of Transnational Community Forms and Their Impact on Immigrant Incorporation." Paper presented at the University of California Comparative Immigration and Integration Program Research Workshop, Center for U.S.–Mexican Studies, University of California, San Diego, February 19.

———. 2000. "Two Nations Under God? Latino Religious Life in the U.S." Typescript.

López Castro, Gustavo. 1986. *La casa dividida: un estudio de caso sobre la migración a Estados Unidos en un pueblo michoacano*. Zamora: El Colegio de Michoacán.

López Castro, Gustavo, and David Barkin. 1990. "Crisis económica, migración internacional y trabajo en una zona de temporal michoacana: una propuesta para el dilema." Research report financed by the Mexican Population Association. Typescript.

Lozano Ascencio, Fernando. 1993. *Bringing It Back Home: Remittances to Mexico from Migrant Workers in the United States*. Monograph Series, no. 37. La Jolla: Center for U.S.–Mexican Studies, University of California, San Diego.

Mahler, Sarah J. 1998. "Theoretical and Empirical Contributions toward a Research Agenda for Transnationalism." In *Transnational-*

ism from Below, edited by Michael Peter Smith and Luis Eduardo Guarnizo. New Brunswick, N.J.: Transaction.

Marcelli, Enrico A., and Wayne A. Cornelius. n.d. "The Changing Profile of Mexican Migrants to the United States: New Evidence from California and Mexico," *Latin American Research Review,* forthcoming 2001.

Marshall, T. H. 1992. *Citizenship and Social Class.* London: Pluto.

Martínez Saldaña, Jesús. 1993. "At the Periphery of Democracy: The Binational Politics of Mexican Immigrants in Silicon Valley." Ph.D. dissertation, University of California, Berkeley.

Massey, Douglas, Rafael Alarcón, Jorge Durand, and Humberto González. 1987. *Return to Aztlán: The Social Process of International Migration from Western Mexico.* Berkeley: University of California Press.

Massey, Douglas, Luin Goldring, and Jorge Durand. 1994. "Continuities in Transnational Migration: An Analysis of Nineteen Mexican Communities," *American Journal of Sociology* 99 (6): 1492–1533.

McDonnell, Patrick. 1995. "Economic Shocks South of Border Resound in Lennox," *Los Angeles Times,* June 20.

Mexican Migration Project. 1999. University of Pennsylvania. On-line. http://lexis.pop.upenn.edu/mexmig.

Mines, Richard. 1981. *Developing a Community Tradition of Migration: A Field Study in Rural Zacatecas, Mexico, and California Settlement Areas.* Monograph Series, no. 3. La Jolla: Program in U.S.–Mexican Studies, University of California, San Diego.

Molinar Horcasitas, Juan. 1999. "Una aproximación al caso de México." Paper presented at the University of California Comparative Immigration and Integration Program Research Workshop, Center for U.S.–Mexican Studies, University of California, San Diego, February 19.

Mummert, Gail. 1999. "Fronteras fragmentadas: identidades múltiples." In *Fronteras fragmentadas,* edited by Gail Mummert. Zamora: El Colegio de Michoacán.

Nagengast, Carole, and Michael Kearney. 1990. "Mixtec Ethnicity: Social Identity, Political Consciousness, and Political Activism," *Latin American Research Review* 25 (2): 61–91.

Ochoa Serrano, Álvaro. 1998. *Viajes de michoacanos al norte.* Zamora: El Colegio de Michoacán.

———. 1999. *Jiquilpan-Huanimban: una historia confinada.* Morelia: Morevallado.

Oldfield, Adrian. 1998. "Citizenship and Community: Civic Republicanism and the Modern World." In *The Citizenship Debates*, edited by Gershon Shafir. Minneapolis: University of Minnesota Press.

Olivo, Antonio, and Chris Kraul. 2000. "L.A. Man Shows Clout of Mexican Expatriates," *Los Angeles Times*, July 10.

Orsi, Robert Anthony. 1985. *The Madonna of 115th Street*. New Haven, Conn.: Yale University Press.

Pérez Godoy, Mara S. 1998. "Social Movements and International Migration: The Mexican Diaspora Seeks Inclusion in Mexico's Political Affairs, 1968–1998." Ph.D. dissertation, University of Chicago.

Plan de Desarrollo Municipal: Sahuayo 1999–2001. 1999. Sahuayo, Michoacán: H. Ayuntamiento Constitucional.

Pocock, J. G. A. 1998. "The Ideal of Citizenship since Classical Times." In *The Citizenship Debates*, edited by Gershon Shafir. Minneapolis: University of Minnesota Press.

Portes, Alejandro. 1999. "Conclusion: Towards a New World: The Origins and Effects of Transnational Activities," *Ethnic and Racial Studies* 22 (2): 462–77.

Portes, Alejandro, Luis E. Guarnizo, and Patricia Landolt. 1999. "The Study of Transnationalism: Pitfalls and Promise of an Emergent Research Field," *Ethnic and Racial Studies* 22 (2): 217–37.

Prado Sánchez, José. 1976. *Sahuayo: tradiciones y leyendas*. Sahuayo, Mich.: n.p.

Program for Mexican Communities Abroad. 1999. Internet System of the Presidency. Mexico. On-line. http://world.presidencia.gob.mx/pages/library/od_mexcommunities.html.

Reichert, Joshua. 1982. "A Town Divided: Economic Stratification and Social Relations in a Mexican Migrant Community," *Social Problems* 29 (4): 411–23.

Rionda Ramírez, Luis Miguel. 1992. *Y jalaron pa'l norte...: migración, agrarismo y agricultura en un pueblo michoacano: Copándaro de Jiménez*. Mexico City: Instituto Nacional de Antropología e Historia.

Ríos, Palmira. 1992. "Comments on Rethinking Migration: A Transnational Perspective." In *Towards a Transnational Perspective on Migration: Race, Class, Ethnicity and Nationalism Reconsidered*, edited by Nina Glick Schiller, Linda Basch, and Cristina Blanc-Szanton. New York: New York Academy of Sciences.

Rivera Salgado, Gaspar. 1999. "Migration and Political Activism: Mexican Transnational Indigenous Communities in a Comparative Perspective." Ph.D. dissertation, University of California, Santa Cruz.

Roberts, Bryan R., et al. 1999. "Transnational Migrant Communities and Mexican Migration to the US," *Ethnic and Racial Studies* 22 (2): 238–66.

Robles et al. 1997. "Se cierra una válvula de escape," *El Financiero Internacional*, April 7.

Rodríguez, Bertha. 1999. "Apoyo a la consulta zapatista," *El Oaxaqueño*, February 28.

Rodríguez, Néstor. 1996. "The Battle for the Border: Notes on Autonomous Migration, Transnational Communities, and the State," *Social Justice* 23 (3): 21–37.

Rouse, Roger. 1989. "Mexican Migration to the United States: Family Relations in the Development of a Transnational Migrant Circuit." Ph.D. dissertation, Stanford University.

————. 1992. "Making Sense of Settlement: Class Transformation, Cultural Struggle, and Transnationalism among Mexican Migrants in the United States." In *Towards a Transnational Perspective on Migration: Race, Class, Ethnicity and Nationalism Reconsidered*, edited by Nina Glick Schiller, Linda Basch, and Cristina Blanc-Szanton. New York: New York Academy of Sciences.

————. 1995. "Thinking through Transnationalism: Notes on the Cultural Politics of Class Relations in the Contemporary United States," *Public Culture* 7: 353–402.

Salinas de Gortari, Carlos. 1982. *Political Participation, Public Investment, and Support for the System: A Comparative Study of Rural Communities in Mexico*. Research Report Series, no. 35. La Jolla: Center for U.S.–Mexican Studies, University of California, San Diego.

Sánchez, George J. 1993. *Becoming Mexican American: Ethnicity, Culture and Identity in Chicano Los Angeles, 1900–1945*. New York: Oxford University Press.

Santamaría Gómez, Arturo. 1994. *La política entre México y Aztlán*. Culiacán: Universidad Autónoma de Sinaloa.

Sheridan, Mary Beth. 1998. "Candidates from Mexico Go Stumping in Southland," *Los Angeles Times*, July 31.

————. 2000. "Mexican Candidates Look to the U.S. for Swing Votes," *Los Angeles Times*, May 5.

Shklar, Judith N. 1991. *American Citizenship: The Quest for Inclusion*. Cambridge, Mass.: Harvard University Press.

Smart, Alan, and Josephine Smart. 1998. "Transnational Social Networks and Negotiated Identities in Interactions between Hong Kong and China." In *Transnationalism from Below*, edited by Michael Peter Smith and Luis Eduardo Guarnizo. New Brunswick, N.J.: Transaction.

Smith, Michael Peter, and Luis Eduardo Guarnizo. 1998. "Theorizing Transnationalism." In *Transnationalism from Below*, edited by Michael Peter Smith and Luis Eduardo Guarnizo. New Brunswick, N.J.: Transaction.

Smith, Robert Courtney. 1995. "Los Ausentes Siempre Presentes: The Imagining, Making and Politics of a Transnational Migrant Community between Ticuani, Puebla, Mexico and New York City." Ph.D. dissertation, Colombia University.

———. 1998a. "Transnational Localities: Community, Technology and the Politics of Membership within the Context of Mexico and U.S. Migration." In *Transnationalism from Below*, edited by Michael Peter Smith and Luis Eduardo Guarnizo. New Brunswick, N.J.: Transaction.

———. 1998b. "Thick and Thin Membership within a Transnational Public Sphere: Diasporic Politics at Home, Domestic Politics Abroad, and the Program for Mexican Communities Abroad." Paper presented at the Willen Seminar, Barnard College, October 26.

Sontag, Deborah. 1998. "A Mexican Town That Transcends All Borders," *New York Times*, July 21.

Sontag, Deborah, and Celia W. Dugger. 1998. "The New Immigrant Tide: A Shuttle between Worlds," *New York Times*, July 19.

Sorenson, Ninna Nyberg. 1998. "Narrating Identity across Dominican Worlds." In *Transnationalism from Below*, edited by Michael Peter Smith and Luis Eduardo Guarnizo. New Brunswick, N.J.: Transaction.

SourceMex. 2000. "Expatriates Sent US $5.9 Billion in Remittances to Mexico in 1999," vol. 11 (14): April 12.

Soysal, Yasemin Nuhoglu. 1994. *Limits of Citizenship: Migrants and Postnational Membership in Europe*. Chicago: University of Chicago Press.

Steller, Tim. 2000. "Part-time Tucsonan Loses Race for Mexican Congress," *Arizona Daily Star*, July 6.

Taylor, Charles. 1992. *Multiculturalism and the Politics of Recognition*. Princeton, N.J.: Princeton University Press.

Tölölyan, Khachig. 1996. "Rethinking *Diaspora*(s): Stateless Power in the Transnational Moment," *Diaspora* 5 (1): 3–35.

Uhlaner, Carole J. 1996. "Latinos and Ethnic Politics in California: Participation and Preference." In *Latino Politics in California*, edited by Aníbal Yáñez-Chávez. La Jolla: Center for U.S.–Mexican Studies, University of California, San Diego.

Vargas González, Pablo. 1993. *Lealtades de la sumisión. Caciquismo: poder local y regional en la Ciénega de Chapala, Michoacán*. Zamora: El Colegio de Michoacán.

Waldinger, Roger, and Mehdi Bozorgmehr, eds. 1996. *Ethnic Los Angeles*. New York: Russell Sage Foundation.

Walker, Lynne. 1999. "Transplanting Success," *San Diego Union-Tribune*, January 10.

Walzer, Michael. 1992. *What It Means to be an American*. New York: Marsilio.

Wiest, Raymond. 1979. "Implications of International Labor Migration for Mexican Rural Development." In *Migration across Frontiers: Mexico and the United States*, edited by Fernando Camara and Robert Van Kemper. Albany: State University of New York.

Woodman Colby, Catherine Letitia. 1998. "Return Migration from Canada and the United States: Its Effects in the Mixteca Alta of Oaxaca, Mexico." Ph.D. dissertation, Vanderbilt University.

Young, Iris Marion. 1989. "Polity and Group Difference: A Critique of the Ideal of Universal Citizenship," *Ethics* 99 (2): 263–90.

Zabin, Carol, and Luis Escala Rabadán. 1998. "Mexican Hometown Associations and Mexican Immigrant Political Empowerment in Los Angeles." Nonprofit Sector Research Fund Working Paper Series. Washington, D.C.: Aspen Institute.

Zendejas-Romero, Sergio. 1998. "Migración de mexicanos a Estados Unidos y su impacto político en los poblados de origen." In *Migración y fronteras*, edited by Manuel Ángel Castillo, Alfredo Lattes, and Jorge Santibáñez. Tijuana: El Colegio de la Frontera Norte.

Zendejas-Romero, Sergio, and Gail Mummert. 1998. "Beyond the Agrarian Question: The Cultural Politics of Ejido Natural Resources." In *The Transformation of Rural Mexico: Reforming the Ejido Sector*, edited by Wayne A. Cornelius and David Myhre. La Jolla: Center for U.S.–Mexican Studies, University of California, San Diego.

Zepeda Patterson, Jorge. 1989. "Sahuayo y Jiquilpan: génesis de la rivalidad por una región 1880–1930." In *Estudios Michoacanos III*, edited by Sergio Zendejas. Zamora: El Colegio de Michoacán.

———. 1990. *Michoacán: sociedad, economía, política y cultura*. Mexico City: Universidad Nacional Autónoma de México.

Zolberg, Aristide R. 1996. "Immigration and Multiculturalism in the Industrial Democracies." In *The Challenge of Diversity: Integration and Pluralism in Societies of Immigration*, edited by Rainer Bauböck, Agnes Heller, and Aristide R. Zolberg. Aldershot, England: Avebury.

Acronyms

CONAPO	Consejo Nacional de Población / National Population Council
EU	European Union
EZLN	Ejército Zapatista de Liberación Nacional / Zapatista Army of National Liberation
FIOB	Frente Indígena Oaxaqueño Binacional / Binational Indigenous Oaxacan Front
HTA	hometown association
IFE	Instituto Federal Electoral / Federal Electoral Institute
INS	U.S. Immigration and Naturalization Service
OMD	Organización de Mexicanos para la Democracia / Organization of Mexicans for Democracy
PACME	Programa para las Comunidades Mexicanos en el Extranjero / Program for Mexican Communities Abroad
PAN	Partido Acción Nacional / National Action Party
PLM	Partido Liberal Mexicano / Mexican Liberal Party
PRD	Partido de la Revolución Democrática / Party of the Democratic Revolution
PRI	Partido Revolucionario Institucional / Institutional Revolutionary Party
PRONASOL	Programa Nacional de Solidaridad / National Solidarity Program
PVEM	Partido Verde Ecologista de México / Green Party of Mexico
SRE	Secretaría de Relaciones Exteriores / Ministry of Foreign Relations

About the Author

David S. Fitzgerald is a Ph.D. candidate in the Department of Sociology at the University of California, Los Angeles, and a Research Associate of the Center for Comparative Immigration Studies at the University of California, San Diego. He received his M.A. in Latin American Studies from the University of California, San Diego. He previously worked as a professional photographer for the *Los Angeles Times*. His principal research interest is Mexican migration to the United States, and he has done fieldwork among migrants in the Mexican state of Michoacán as well as southern California, supported by the Tinker Foundation. He has published on Mexican immigration in the *Journal of Social Work Research and Evaluation*.